DIRT
ROADS
TO
RUNWAYS

DIRT ROADS TO RUNWAYS

DEFENDING THE AMERICAN DREAM
FOR THE NEXT GENERATION

KEITH GROSS

Foreword by Roger Stone

ILLUMIFY
MEDIA.COM

Published by
Illumify Media Global
www.IllumifyMedia.com
"Let's bring your book to life!"

Paperback ISBN: 978-1-959099-77-2

Cover design by Debbie Lewis

Printed in the United States of America

CONTENTS

FOREWORD

KEITH GROSS BELIEVES IN the American Dream because he has lived the American Dream. Born under modest circumstances, through grit, hard work, and innovation, Keith Gross made enough money to be able to retire at a young age and never have to work again.

He could literally go fishing. Taking the broader view, however, rather than retiring to a life of luxury and privilege, Keith has rededicated himself to preserving the promise of the American Dream that worked out for him so well. Others may choose the easier path, but not Keith Gross. He wants future Americans to have the freedoms and the opportunity that allowed him to succeed.

Like all Americans, Keith sees what is happening in America circa 2023. They describe America as a systematically racist nation; they appoint Marxists and other radical ideologues to positions of power; they allow millions to surge across our Southern Border; they're still attempting to federalize our election systems and processes; they've implemented critical race theory in our schools, our military, and across the entire U.S. government; and all along, they've raised the national debt which now exceeds $30 trillion—spending us toward extinction.

Keith recognizes the Afghanistan disaster, the myriad lies about COVID, a certain Biden-owned laptop, a complete refusal to investigate allegations of election irregularities, the war in the Middle East, Americans still held hostage, the war in Ukraine, "peaceful" pro-Palestinian protests on our streets based on one-sided media manipulation, all while China gets a pass.

Like many Americans, Keith Gross understands that we are approaching the breaking point, that we can no longer tolerate Big Tech companies which censor us, U.S. government intelligence agencies which illegally spy on us, and a judicial system that targets parents simply for showing up at school board meetings to express concern about the curriculum being taught to their children.

At the same time, Keith understands that an America that is $30 trillion in debt cannot continue to just print money and ship it to foreign countries to wage wars in which America's inherent interests are less than clear, nor can we continue to tax hardpressed working American families to pay for these foreign wars in which they honestly have no stake.

One of the things you will learn in this book is that Keith Gross clearly understands that Washington D.C. is broken and that we cannot rely on career-politicians of either party to bring real solutions to America's problems. The system urgently needs true outsiders and independent thinkers like Keith Gross.

Keith Gross clearly appreciates that it is extremely difficult to trust this current administration on any level, especially when they lie with a straight face to the American people on a daily basis. Keith understands that anyone who questions these rotten foreign and domestic policies are demonized as racist, an Islamophobe, homophobe or whatever-o-phobe. But fortunately, as he outlines in this volume, Keith is fearless and determined.

Keith Gross also sees the continuation of the unleashing of the federal government on citizens who are simply exercising their constitutional rights and the establishment media covers all this incompetence with a fake smile due to their own deep corruption.

Keith Gross clearly understands that he cannot retire or stand down while our president rarely entertains questions or takes responsibility for his tone deafness and failures, and that this White House ignores any questions about America's legitimate security concerns. He sees that we have yet to hear from the President of the United States an explanation of any U.S. national security interests for any of these failures in Ukraine, the Middle East, at the border, rising crime, and a failing economy.

Above all, Keith Gross understands that Americans must take a stand at their local levels and get involved where they can, with what they can, when they can. No more excuses. Keith Gross can be counted on to be on the front lines in this fight.

Therefore, Keith Gross has decided to take a stand. He understands that the struggle to preserve our basic constitutional liberties is today, and, rather than choose a life of luxury and comfort, he has elected to fight for America's survival and renewal.

Keith Gross' story reminds me of Theodore Roosevelt's famous remarks about the man in the arena:

"It is not the critic who counts; not the man who points out how the strong man stumbles, or where the doer of deeds could have done them better. The credit belongs to the man who is actually in the arena, whose face is marred by dust and sweat and blood; who strives valiantly; who errs, who comes short again and again, because there is no effort without error and short-coming; but who does actually strive to do the deeds; who knows the great enthusiasms, the great devotions; who spends himself in a worthy cause; who at the best knows in the end the triumph of high achievement, and who at the worst, if he fails, at least fails while daring greatly, so that his place shall never be with those cold and timid souls who neither know victory nor defeat." Keith is the man in the arena. Keith understands that there can be no victory without effort, and no victory for America without risk.

This is the manifesto of Keith Gross, an entrepreneur, businessman and patriot, who has decided that America is worth fighting for. Like the Founding Fathers, the majority of whom were young men risking everything in the fight for freedom, Keith

Gross is putting everything on the line. The question you must ask yourself after reading this important book, is whether you are prepared to stand and fight beside him.

ROGER STONE
Fort Lauderdale, Florida

INTRODUCTION

BY CURRENT AVERAGES, I will reach the fifty-yard line of my life by the time this book is published. Sure, many live beyond 80, but I'd rather write about the first chapter now with the hope that readers will find it both enjoyable and helpful. Entrepreneurs are risk takers by nature, and anyone considering business as a calling finds the experiences of others—both successes and failures—useful when blazing their own trails.

Without pretending to be a champion or expert of anything, it's been said that I've lived something of an accelerated life and have reached uncommon levels of success, having started with a set of uncommon circumstances. While I don't plan to abandon my current practice of business acquisition, creation, systemization, or the development of strategies, I do plan to set out on another course of action and devote most of my time and energy to public service.

The purpose of this autobiography is to tell you how I got to this point, and hopefully provide some entertainment with personal stories of growth that leave others with a sense of optimism, inspiration, and new energy to fuel their own contributions to the fabric of American life. After all, life is supposed to be shared, in my opinion. We learn when the road is shared with others, stories are told, and ideas come to life. I have spent some time in public service as a member of the Army National Guard, a law clerk at the United States Department of Justice, and briefly as a prosecutor for the state of Florida. This time will be different—I'll need to run a campaign for U.S. Senate in the state of Florida. Many understand that running for any political office today is a sort of self-punishment—so then, why?

I believe that when you cross a finish line or achieve a milestone, you have an obligation to turn around and help others who are still in the race. While so many politicians find themselves tangled in nests of corruption, I can't be bought. That's why I've worked hard to forge success in business. From my humble beginnings, I already know I don't need much of anything to survive in the first place, so I'm ready to start building the next chapter—one of public service—to concentrate on improving the lives of others through better governance, better policies, and a strengthened Republic.

Political campaigns have become riddled with vindictive tactics, are expensive, and are often fraught with cheating, all of which are some of the many things that pointed me toward the decision to run. We simply cannot continue to accept a political environment in which only the rich, leveraged, corrupt, or installed run our country. That means that while it is risky and punishing, honest and authentic candidates must run. In business, I've often said that if you want it done right, just do it yourself. That appears to be increasingly applicable to politics.

When I was growing up, I felt free, patriotic, and confident about my future. Today, politicians seem to breed distrust, dismiss the will of the people, and hunger for power. Instead of worrying about the future of our country and listening to the concerns of the people who are truly supposed to direct our course, they worry about things like the *"narrative"* and *"optics."*

It strikes me that any representative who is just doing their job, working hard on behalf of their constituents, and being honest, shouldn't have to actively worry about such things. Appearances and messaging ought to take care of themselves when honesty, clarity, courage, and diligence are applied to the faithful execution of any office.

We need to restore common sense in government and policy, civility in public discourse, and honest, true transparency for the citizens of our country. We need to remember that what remains of the free world depends on our example and leadership. After all, if America fails, freedom fails around the globe. Government is not a tool to dictate the choices people make. It is a tool we should use to preserve rights and freedoms, chief among which is the right to make individual choices. Instead of mandating health protocols, we need to inject citizens with renewed optimism, faith in government, and to foster the freedoms every individual needs in order to create and follow their dreams.

The "American Dream" is a collective dream to light the path for all of civilization. Unfortunately, instead of nurturing the fragile freedom and lifeblood of Western Civilization, too many of today's policies trespass on our rights and trample our very souls, sapping individuality in an unending power grab by government.

So, here's the story of where my journey began, where I stand today, and how I intend to continue to move forward down the field toward the goal post.

1

THE EARLY YEARS—MY VIEW FROM A TRAILER

AS A CHILD, I first saw the world through the windows of a double wide trailer home in Southport, Florida. There was a pond good for fishing in the back, on a rural four acres. We raised chickens and had a horse and an ATV to move around the property. It wasn't a trailer in a trailer park, it was just a trailer home on a piece of land in the middle of Florida's panhandle region. The town is actually called Southport, which is different from the city of South Port near Orlando. We lived just outside of Panama City, so I usually just say that I'm from there because most people have never heard of Southport.

Our family, which became four once my sister, Kimberly, was born five years after me, enjoyed camping and boating on lakes in rural North Florida. Often, we were accompanied by grandparents and friends, or met acquaintances at various campsites. Nothing was ever fancy, but it was always fun. My mother was always home, but she handled the books for the small businesses my parents operated. Each year, one of the businesses sponsored my baseball team. So, while not rich or famous, we had some visibility and were active in our community and church. We lived on New Church Road and drove our riding mower to cut the grass at the church where my mother was also a Sunday School teacher.

In 1983, the year I was born, Southport was barely on any maps. The rural area was just a place where people lived, farmed, worked, and gathered. In 1983, all of Bay County, with an expansive area of 1033 square miles, was home to just 106,697 residents. In 2020, the population was recorded at 175,216—significant, but not staggering. Southport remains unincorporated, and in 2020 registered a population of just 11,059, or 39.8 people per square mile, which is about double the population in 1980.

The entire territory of Florida, which became a state in 1845, was purchased for $5 Million in 1821. Andrew Jackson was appointed by President James Monroe to become the first Military Governor. The largest "real city" near Southport was Panama City, incorporated in 1913. The adjacent and very popular Panama City Beach wasn't incorporated until 1971. Even if you google Southport today, there's a good chance you'll be directed to a different area, a neighborhood near Kissimmee, named South Port (with a space), on the south shore of Lake Tohopekaliga.

This is a bit of a long way to explain that Southport wasn't center stage in America, Florida, or even Bay County. Perhaps that's why clearer heads still prevail in the area. I'd like to think that common sense was more common in Southport, and it may well be true. Nobody cared if you did or didn't eat meat. Most would find the subject a really weird thing to want to discuss. Nobody cared about which pop artists or movie stars were on the covers of tabloids. Nobody flaunted designer labels, and it's likely nobody owned any.

Growing up in Southport was a boy's dream—I was free to explore, get dirty, catch fish, ride around on a four-wheeler, and tend to the chickens and other tasks as best I could. I helped my parents with whatever I was asked to do. Their lives were not so dreamy given the several tough businesses they owned and operated, none of them highly profitable. Making ends meet was a struggle, but they did better than most in the community. Their companies included land clearing, a small trucking company, and a local gas station. A good-sized garden along with the chickens helped keep food on the table.

We never felt poor, underprivileged, "at risk," or any of the other labels the government likes to place on people they've never met. Any burden felt by the adults in my family was largely shielded from my sister and me, and the other adults I knew were equally prudent. We felt blessed and loved. Our family was quite self-sufficient. Minds were focused on what needed doing next, and our community wasn't filled with "victims," but rather with hard working people who just might have to drive a bit further for some needed goods or services.

In the south, most days are hot and humid. A garden can seemingly become a jungle overnight. Weeding was a daily task, but the rewards were tremendous. Entire days in harvest season would be spent "puttin' up" food. Everyone pitched in until the job was done. Each crop required different handling. It's likely I acquired enough information to run my own farm, restaurant, or grocery store just watching what happened at home and doing what was asked of me. I certainly learned to cook, too. While ours was just a larger property with an oversized garden and chicken coop, my grandparents and great grandfather operated actual farms. Heading over to help either of them was a regular part of my life as a child and teen.

At our property, we grew tomatoes, corn, okra, beans, peas, onions, squash, greens, carrots, and peppers of various kinds, as well as cantaloupe, honeydew, and watermelon. It wasn't always easy to keep up with the fast growth. After storing or eating what we could, my mother would often load up a wagon and we'd walk to pull the excess food to country neighbors who were always grateful. Country neighbors are like that—they share excess food, borrow or lend tools, and enjoy conversations. I'm sure that's true for neighbors in most places, but in Southport, it took a little effort to cover several miles in order to reach a few friendly driveways on foot.

There was always a way to provide, prepare for the future, repair almost anything that was broken, help others, and stay positive. Some weekends, while at my grandparents' farm, I'd be staring at a mountain of corn on the table and every counter of the kitchen, with more in bushels on the floor, more filling the entire floor of a screened porch, and still more covering an outdoor porch. And there were acres of corn yet in the field to be harvested.

I'd follow instructions given—using a particular curved knife to strip kernels from cobs—to prepare for canning and freezing. These were family events with my mother, grandparents, uncles, and eventually my sister Kimberly. What seemed an enormous task, perhaps even impossible to a rather young boy, eventually resulted in jars upon jars on endless shelves to feed many people for months to come.

Peas were the next big job. There were mountains of peas, all waiting to be shelled by hand, then blanched and put up in jars. The amount was so great that some were also frozen to stuff large deep freezers. Nobody in my extended family ever had peas or corn on their grocery list, but everyone gave up a few weekends to make that happen. I'm sure many people in America would rather just pick up a few cans at the store, but they should consider how food gets to grocery store shelves in the first place.

Every task had good reason, and the reasons quickly became evident, even to a child. It was all about where food actually comes from and what people need in order to survive. It was also about family, with plenty of time for conversation along with a mix of teaching and learning, depending upon a range of levels of experience.

Still, with all the food production and work, the farm owned by my father's parents was really only a subsistence farm. While it provided many things for them and for their extended family, they were actually very poor and relied upon government food rations to fill out dietary requirements. With two feet of potatoes stored on the floor of a barn, along with some cattle and pigs, they still ate government food rations.

Labels on the food stood out. Silver cans marked "U.S. Government" in a thick black font were impossible to overlook. There was no hiding from the fact that these were provisions from the federal government. It wasn't like today, when even kids can present a card (originally intended to provide essentials to heads of needy households) and present it as though it is an ordinary credit card. My hard-working, farming grandparents had to pick up designated rations of whatever the government decided would suffice, marked "U.S. Government." My grandparents maintained dignity while participating in what today is truly a wasteful program.

The federal government has an odd way of managing agriculture. That probably stems from the fact that few, if any, of our congressional representatives have ever actually farmed or have any clue what is required to grow food. As such, our government does nonsensical things like pay farmers to destroy crops and livestock, or encourage them to not even attempt to grow and sell food.

My mother's grandfather, my great grandfather also had a farm. Theirs was a commercial operation with every animal under the sun. They sold cattle, sugar cane and other products. While there, I learned how to care for pigs and cattle. Working at the farms of both sets of grandparents and my responsibilities at home provided me with an education of the sort that money can't buy. It was customary to remain cheerful, take pride in work, and revere God and nature. Nobody complained. Everyone pitched in until the work was done. Conversations were in person, not electronic. Mistakes were acknowledged and corrected. Truth was truth, lies were lies, facts were facts, and life was good.

Not all the learning was pleasurable. Animals are not always cute. Crops sometimes fail. And, just as plants are harvested, so must be livestock. What most would find truly horrific (because farmers have always done it for them) becomes a fact of life for those who grow food. It's not pretty, but it's certainly not evil to produce meat and poultry for the benefit of others. Skill is required to be successful as a farmer, and every aspect of farming conducted by those striving for success is deserving of respect. Farmers should rightfully take pride in their work and the results.

Regardless of fads or fashion where food is concerned, humans are omnivores who require carnivorous levels of protein. Most people appreciate a great steak, barbequed ribs, chicken, ham, or Thanksgiving turkey. The idea that we should resort to eating bugs to spare animals or save the planet is just silly. Farmers are perhaps the most humane people on the planet. They care for their land and animals, and have the utmost respect for mother nature. They understand life and help others to stay alive.

Animals, however, are not kind or compassionate toward each other. That, too, is a matter of survival. One thing to understand about chickens, for example, is that there's always something waiting to kill them the moment you turn your back. Most often, there are several things at once. In my youth, I'd sometimes hear a squeal or a howl, perhaps the screech of a hawk. That's how you knew something was trying to kill them.

Today's "critter cams" make it more obvious. Many people are surprised to see photos captured the next day—a raccoon, bobcat, snake, weasel, panther, and the list goes on. If there had been critter cams available on my family's property, it may have picked up images of the panthers we'd often hear at night. Predators are quick to strike. A coyote will grab a chicken and haul it away to a private dinner table.

One of my early and highly uncomfortable life lessons was about chickens. Even though a young hatch of about a dozen chicks were in a crate, inside a coop, and behind a fence surrounding the entire operation, some animal managed to pull every single little leg of each chick through the crate and bite it off.

The sight was highly upsetting and my heart sank. When I ran to the house to report the incident to my mother, she said, "They won't survive. You'll need to go out there and wring their necks."

That was some lesson and some task for an eight-year-old, but she was right. We couldn't watch them suffer and they had no chance of a comfortable, happy life, or of becoming food for anyone. It was better for them to die quickly with compassion than slowly with pain.

While I hated my assignment, I couldn't help but wish I'd gotten there sooner and known what to do without making a trip to the kitchen to consult my mother. Like a cowboy shooting his ailing and beloved horse, it's emotionally painful but necessary to show respect for the animal over one's own emotions. The sooner such a task can be completed, the better.

Of this you can be sure: farmers can never afford to "kick the can down the road," as politicians are often accused of and routinely do. Work is tackled immediately and problems are faced head-on to prevent larger ones from developing. Farmers can't push problems off to escape immediate discomfort while burdening future generations. If a farmer fails to act in a timely manner on any front, the consequences are felt immediately.

In Florida's panhandle region, one quickly also learns that just as chickens face many predators, so do people. Yet, caring for the animals becomes a greater concern than concern for oneself. I recall being sent out at night during storms to retrieve our storm-phobic horse who would customarily just stand frozen under a tree, with instructions to put the horse in the stall. I was terrified each time as I could hear the whistles and screams of panthers at night. One just learns to put fear aside and do what needs to be done. Overcoming fear is necessary for freedom, forward motion, and productivity.

Aside from panthers, Florida is home to nearly every snake you can imagine. Six of the forty-four species of snakes can kill you quickly. They include the southern copperhead, the cottonmouth (also called the water moccasin), the eastern diamondback rattlesnake, the timber rattlesnake, and the dusky pygmy rattlesnake. And then, of course, there are lots of alligators. Oddly, Florida is also the only place on the planet where crocodiles and alligators both thrive.

None of all the things that could kill you kept me or other kids from roaming the woods, venturing into the yard at night, or swimming in the pond, which quickly kicked up mud that impaired vision. It was, however, a likely factor that resulted in me owning my first gun at age four. That's right, age four. It was a "BB" gun. Of course, a BB gun isn't considered a "real" gun, but it was important to learn to shoot and handle firearms at an early age. My first shot gun was a gift received at about age ten, and I've owned several others since. I had an expert teacher in my Army veteran grandfather, who also gifted me several of his guns upon his death.

I almost can't remember when I didn't own a gun. I really can't remember being in any car that wasn't armed with a gun either. Everyone had a gun in their car, and most natives of Florida still do. Not being able to defend yourself or protect your family is considered irresponsible. The wide array of predatory animals provided a very good reason to know how to shoot, but also, if an uninvited, predatory human ever visited properties in the rural areas of the panhandle, anyone would certainly want to have a gun at the ready. That's not because anyone is anxious to shoot anything except food, but because if your house was invaded or you faced some threat, it could take an awfully long time for the sheriff to arrive because of the distances involved.

Nothing I could ever write would keep tourists away from Florida for its glorious flora and fauna, along with famous beaches. I paint this image not to resurrect the wild frontier that it truly once was and, in some respects, still is, but rather to express why I have formed certain political opinions and learned so much outside of my formal education. In short, the phrase "common sense is uncommon" is an understatement, but all the lessons are there—free of charge—for anyone who is willing to merely pay attention.

2

THE LIGHTER SIDE OF LEARNING—FAMILY, FRIENDS, AND FUN

OLD ADAGES CARRY MUCH weight in wisdom. Today, I could write about nearly all of them, but as a child I sometimes had trouble deciphering the things adults would repeat, such as: *"That is like the pot calling the kettle black;"* or, *"Don't cry over spilt milk."* But a favorite is one my mother clearly understood: *"All work and no play makes Jack a dull boy."*

Wisemen have long recommended life shouldn't be all work and no play, and it certainly wasn't for me. The pond on our property was great for fishing. When time permitted, I'd head to the water and try my luck, often with surprising success. Sometimes my mother would ask that I take my sister Kimberly along with me. I really didn't mind, but I did know the chance of success catching anything was greatly reduced. Yet, she provided me with free entertainment.

Young girls tend to become interested and adventurous themselves. They love to laugh, explore, and have fun. And precocious children, like Kimberly and

I were, are very curious. So, aside from making sure she didn't land *in* the pond, there were questions to be answered, distractions to juggle, and big brother tasks to perform if she got herself into any kind of mess. But that's the sort of stuff that creates lasting memories and bonds between siblings. We were grateful to have each other then and remain close today.

In fact, Kimberly should likely take some credit for my interest and success in pursuing a law degree and my work as an attorney. She was the first to teach me a valuable lesson about contract law through her breach of the very first contract I ever wrote. It was about a turtle. I quickly learned to write contracts more tightly.

You see, on one of our joint adventures at the pond, we caught a turtle. We took it home and filled the bathtub to create a habitat. We brought it rocks and plants, minnows, and other fancy stuff. Yet, each night, our mother reminded us to bathe and get ready for bed. We couldn't really do that with the turtle occupying the bathtub, and Kimberly was feeling the heat of dodging mother's bath directive. The turtle was jointly owned, but she didn't want to take on her share of the responsibility. She said the turtle could only live in the bathtub for a few days. So, I wrote up a contract.

We both signed it. It contained something of an NDA. We weren't going to talk about or reveal confidential information about the turtle.

Of course, as you might expect, she spilled the beans. She burst into the living room, and said something like, "Mom, I'm not supposed to tell you, but I have to…There's a turtle living in the bathtub, Keith and I have a secret contract, and that's why we can't bathe!"

That's right, the very first contract I ever wrote blew up in smoke. But, by that time, I really wanted to take a bath myself, so we set the turtle free. Instead of being angry with me, my mother was actually impressed that I'd written a fairly good contract. Nonetheless, I was instructed to scrub the bathroom.

There's really no substitute for the things you learn in real life if you pay attention. Too many people believe they can't learn outside of a formal education. Even parents of young children believe this. That's a damaging trap and it's not true. What is true is that parents are the first and best teachers of their children. Enjoying the fun of a pet turtle for a few days was not worth having to scrub a bathroom top to bottom and haul the former pet back to the pond. Real consequences lead to faster learning.

Adventures with friends were also part of my childhood. Kids in rural areas often learn to do certain things at a young age because they have to, but then they are rewarded with doing them for fun simply because they can. For me, that meant exploring the property with my friends by driving around on an ATV. Four acres isn't a farm, but it's not tiny either. All the neighboring properties were also large. Nobody felt poor, but nobody ever had any money to speak of, so entertainment was simple and likely more rewarding than many things considered luxuries. Testing your skills, such as driving a four-wheeler, was almost always a part of producing solid fun.

We learned confidence, resilience, determination, and a whole host of other life skills from rather ordinary things that ordinary kids did in the 1980's and 90's. Back then, we were free of helicopter parents, helmets, masks, knee pads, etc., and natural consequences taught us these life skills rather quickly.

In many respects, we've become a society which is afraid to let kids be kids. We try to protect kids from absolutely everything during playtime, but then fail to protect them from some things which cause lasting harm. We've invited and welcomed the federal government to protect and instruct children for us instead of taking charge, as parents have the natural right and responsibility to do. We've nearly relinquished parental rights to the federal government. This has led to a predictable move towards indoctrination rather than education. We've even become so complacent that we allowed the federal government to tell our children to wear a mask and instruct them in how to wash their hands. This top-down nanny state and the acceptance of it (because then any mistake is that of the government's and not of individuals) must end. The government, after all, never faces consequences for any mistakes. They just pass them on to you in new regulations and taxes.

3

TURMOIL IN THE TRAILER

MY IDYLLIC CHILDHOOD HIT a temporary roadblock and changed significantly when I was 12. My parents divorced and my father went to jail for multiple crimes—primarily crimes of violence against my mother. I haven't spoken with or seen him since, and I don't intend to.

That may sound callous, but it's not. You see, I've come to understand the plight of many women, the importance of life, and the prevalence of domestic violence, and that law and order are critical to civilized society. My mother had every right to exercise her God given human rights—"*life, liberty, and the pursuit of happiness.*" Certainly, she did it for the benefit of myself and my sister as well.

My mother gave me life in the midst of her own young life. To me, all seemed well, I had everything I needed, and I was loved. She made that happen too—promoted a sense of security and well-being within me. Kids don't know what's really going on in the lives of their parents unless their parents are weak and burden children with things they couldn't (or shouldn't) possibly manage.

Happily, the entire episode began and ended within about six months. At least from my perspective (which I'm sure was incomplete), it was short, and then it was over. Of course, I was shielded from details and I don't really care to dig. But, at my adult age, it's clear to me that the situation was serious—grave enough for my father to have gone to prison, and inexorable enough for my mother to have bravely stood up for herself and pursued a painful and uncertain course of action that threatened to render her alone and penniless.

When people write tales of strong, resourceful women, they should include my mother, Rhonda. She was just 18 years of age when she found herself expecting me, and as such, hadn't yet acquired any higher education or employment history outside of the family businesses. The businesses were successful enough at the time, but they all went out of business. Post-divorce, my mother could no longer maintain the cost of our home, so we temporarily moved in to live with my mother's parents.

Until quite recently, to be a young mother was considered normal in both the United States and the rest of the world. In more recent, postmodern, materialistic generations of "me, myself, and I," "Ivy League" types plan weddings for their debutantes and Princeton grads, with price tags of hundreds of thousands of dollars. They eagerly flaunt their materialistic celebrations in popular social magazines, but often discourage young motherhood.

The lucrative education industry promotes the notion that individuals are worthless and that females, most especially, will die on the vine unless they possess higher education degrees and have already established a "career," or at least have some impressive job title before they wed or have children. Their goal is to increase profit margins and produce graduates who often don't know how to actually do much of anything. It has had a devastating effect on birth rates. More babies, not fewer, are needed to maintain a healthy economy, society, and environment. The world wasn't built on a stack of white papers and dissertations.

Industry in America longs for people skilled in trades. Without them, we don't have enough people to build, fix, or invent things. For the most part, the real world has kept humming because those who value life support the lives of others, particularly babies, before worrying about their own long-term futures or appearances. They have faith. They share their lives, sacrifice, and care for their newborns and the elderly, along with whatever else life hands to them.

Any disadvantage that my mother may have had following the divorce was reversed quickly through her hard work and determination. She put herself through school while working as a park ranger, built her own house on a property adjacent to my grandparents, earned a teaching degree, then taught before being promoted to school principal. And she still managed to earn a master's degree in mathematics while working full time.

Her eventual retirement from the position of school principal didn't last very long. She now owns and operates her own franchise in the home insulation industry, through the company my spouse and I founded. When I was just developing that franchise, following the sale of a truck washing company, she was chomping at the bit and expressed an interest in owning her own business. She got remarried to a professional several years ago who is also a military veteran and engineer—a career history which now seems something of a family tradition.

In hindsight, the "turmoil in the trailer" seems a blip on the screen. Thankfully, I seem to have inherited my mother's ambition and grit. She often said that I didn't like to sit idle, and that's certainly true. One of her favorite stories to tell is that of me single handedly building a new trail for more efficient travel on our original property.

She's right. I was restless and looking for something to do, so, I took my small 18" hatchet and took down a row of pine trees through the property to make a trail. My hands were blistered and bloody, but now we had a quick and easy path to areas we needed to take care of on the property. She was quite pleased, and I resolved to save up any allowance money to buy a bigger axe.

4

DOWN ANOTHER DIRT ROAD

SO, OFF WE WENT with our belongings to live with my grandparents, Terry and Jeanette Porter, who really were a short quarter mile away down another Southport dirt road. They had a larger country lot, too—four or five acres. Their property didn't have a garden but did have a branch of the nearby river bend through it, which provided interesting areas to explore. The branch leads east to the very large Dear Point Lake. Between the two, my habit of hunting for fish would see no immediate end.

Once some of the dust settled, my mother got to work building a new home for us on the property adjacent to my grandparents so we wouldn't live with them indefinitely. It's fair to say she "hit the ground running" to piece together everything our family of three required to regain comfort, stability, independence, and freedom.

Before moving in with my grandparents, I had already spent considerable time at their home to help them complete various tasks, somewhat of a necessity as my grandfather was wheelchair bound for my entire life. It was somewhat of a blessing for me that he was in a wheelchair because it meant that I spent more time with him than I otherwise likely would have. He had a brilliant mind and was a real-life rocket scientist.

He served in the Army as an engineer and was stationed in Germany with a basecamp in Huntsville, Alabama, where he worked on the Redstone Missile program. No less than the very famous Wernher von Braun, who was a German aerospace engineer and space architect, was the technical director of the program. Although my grandfather was only about 18 or 19 and probably never laid eyes on him except perhaps from some distance or in a photo hung in a hallway, everyone at Redstone was aware of von Braun and the team of former Nazi scientists who worked there.

You may wonder how and why, during and following WWII, any American Army Engineer was working with a former German Nazi who was responsible for developing Germany's "miracle weapon"—a payload that could be delivered using a rocket or missile named the V2.

After WWI, Germany was not allowed to use ships or planes to deliver missiles. However, nothing in the post war treaty banned missiles delivered by rockets—likely because few, if any, had dreamt of the possibility. Wernher von Braun had dreamt not of bombs, but of rockets since his teens. He was later conscripted into the Nazi Party and SS to develop rockets bearing artillery loads for Hitler. He was the premier scientist in the field and was successful in developing and launching the V2 rocket, but his success came rather late in the war.

Once it was clear to von Braun that Germany would be defeated and occupied, he surrendered to the US in 1944, convincing many on his team of scientists to join him. Having lived through his native country's defeat in two world wars, his explanation for switching sides was that he wanted to join the winners.

Von Braun was warmly welcomed by the US, and then worked with the US Army for the next fifteen years, assigned to the development of ballistic missiles and the military operation, "Project Paperclip." Along with his team of former Nazi scientists, he was installed at Fort Bliss, Texas, and assisted in launches of the V2 at White Sands Missile Range in New Mexico, where my grandfather and his team would conduct annual test launches of the rockets they operated.

Five years later, von Braun and his team were sent to Huntsville, Alabama, to work at the Redstone Arsenal. There, the team developed the Army's Redstone and Jupiter ballistic missiles, the Jupiter C, Juno II, and Saturn I launch vehicles.

After 10 years of working at the Redstone Arsenal, President Eisenhower transferred rocket development from the Army to the newly established National Aeronautics and Space Administration (NASA) and appointed von Braun its first Director of the Marshall Space Flight Center. He was also the chief architect of the Saturn V Launch Vehicle, which was the super booster that would propel Alan Shepard on a suborbital flight as the first American astronaut.

This is what truly launched the US space program toward eventual success and the first lunar landing. Soon after, President John F. Kennedy announced his goal of sending a man to the moon. On July 20, 1969, that mission was fulfilled. Wernher von Braun made it happen and was at President Kennedy's side when it did.

These are the types of stories my grandfather would relay to me while simultaneously walking me through some complicated mechanical or electrical tasks that needed doing. He followed all the developments in space exploration and the interests of Elon Musk, who truly *became* our space program in 2002 with his investment in research and development, and founding of Space X.

Now, I'm not trying to claim that I was wheeling Stephen Hawking around listening to scientific histories and technical explanations, but my experience with my grandfather and his detailed stories were likely the closest thing to it that ever happened to anyone in Southport, Florida.

My grandfather's physical disabilities, however, were not service or military related. After service, he worked as a chemical engineer at a large chemical company in central Florida where sadly, one day, an overhead pipe containing boiling hot 98 percent concentrated sulfuric acid burst, leaving the caustic chemical to burn through his clothing and much of his skin. His face wasn't disfigured, but the rest of his body certainly was, and he spent months at a burn center in Georgia undergoing various treatments and a series of skin grafts.

But the chemical accident wasn't responsible for the loss of use of his legs. That came later when he was thrown off a motorcycle and fractured his spine. My mother was only seven years old when that happened, so I only ever knew him in a wheelchair. Still, his mind was brilliant. From him, I came to understand the power of positive thinking. He didn't act like a victim of any sort, didn't talk about anything he couldn't do, and only set his mind to what needed doing and how it would get done.

Even before we moved in with my grandparents, I installed a ceiling fan at their home—start to finish—at age 9. Grandpa and I got into the car, headed to the local hardware store, and picked up the fan. From there I unboxed it, with grandpa in his chair next to a ladder, then made a series of trips up and down the ladder while following his instructions word for word, until it was completely installed.

A broken ceiling fan in Florida was considered a top priority, as my grandmother could not stand the heat. She ruled the roost, so it was an urgent matter. The ceiling fan was just the start. Then there was the car, the riding mower, other fixtures and machinery, and anything else electrical or mechanical. I'd be doing it with my grandfather instructing me every step of the way. Again, free education and I'd rather be fixing a problem than sitting idle anyway.

Every visit to my grandparents' house was fun because my grandmother was a quintessential Southern woman who would try to feed you the moment you entered the house. After some success with a meal, she would also have about three meals for any visitor to take along with them when they left. She often worried out loud that my naturally skinny self was "wasting away" and that I "ought to eat more biscuits and gravy," while also hollering to my grandfather that he'd better be careful or he'd get me electrocuted. I often had to work to suppress a belly laugh until either she or grandpa laughed first.

All of this experience with my grandfather spurred my interest in science and eventually convinced me to register my first major in college as electrical engineering. As we settled into our new multi-generational living arrangements, I kept working and learning from my grandfather, looking after my sister, and helping in any other way possible as a teenaged student, while my mother absolutely attacked the job of putting her own life together to support all of us.

Although she described me as not one to enjoy sitting idle, it was nearly impossible to do so even if so inclined while watching her determination and commitment. We both took on a life of school, work, sleep, repeat, but left time for faith, family, friends, and fun. I'm thin, not because I don't eat enough, but because I'm genetically wired to keep moving—probably because of my mother and grandfather.

Once comfortable in our new routine, it seemed time for me to venture out to make some money on my own, even though I wasn't quite old enough. At 13, I took on the job of showing up every day at the local gas station and convenience store, "Big Bucks," to learn what I'd be asked to do there for cash. They couldn't actually hire me until age 14, which they did when the time came. My grandmother already worked there, so we weren't exactly strangers, and it was more than a convenience store in Southport. It was the everything-you-need-and-only-place-you-might-be-able-to-get-it store for miles around.

5

THE VALUE OF BUSINESS EDUCATION FROM A GAS STATION

"BIG BUCK'S" IS STILL there—smack in the middle of Southport. It's actually called "Big Buck Food Mart," but everyone during my time there just called it "Big Buck's," and locals still do today. Maybe the name was a reference to needing bucks to buy anything, and that the owner certainly wasn't making big bucks. It could also be acknowledgement of the fact that some folks have big bucks, but they don't live in Southport.

Situated on a couple acres on County Road 2321, it's a gas station, convenience store, and deli, with a real butcher and meat market, too. Locals still rave about the food. Some say they serve the best biscuits and smoked meats in all of Bay County. Many complain about the price of gas, but that's outside the control of local gas stations all across America today.

My job, especially when I was just 13, was whatever I was asked to do. I wasn't a hired employee, but I'd show up before or after school and offer to help. At the end of my "shifts," I'd always be rewarded with some pay—a small cash acknowledgement of appreciation from my grandmother, the owner, or a combination. It was rewarding beyond any weekly allowance for chores because it didn't come from my mom.

During my time there, Big Buck's opened at 5:00 in the morning and closed late at night. I think their hours are similar today. I could easily squeeze in some time outside of the school day and on weekends. I started out helping my grandmother who had already been working there. She'd show me how to clean the meat counter, work the cash register, and stock the shelves. Sometimes I was asked to do things I already knew how to do, like mop the floors and break down boxes. Cleaning up most anything that fell or spilled was generally delegated to me also.

I didn't care what I was asked to do. Work was no stranger to me, and earning money on my own was thrilling, but not because I was earning *big bucks* or that I was eager to spend them. Rather, it was because I couldn't stop thinking about how I could save anything I earned to eventually build my complete financial independence and hopefully, a business of my own.

Most young people and employees feared the gruff owner of Big Buck's, James Spikes, but frequented or worked at the establishment anyway. Mr. Spikes wasn't particularly friendly to most, but he was friendly to me. Perhaps he simply tolerated me more than others. Unlike some other employees, I always paid attention to what he was doing and asked him about it. I was careful not to interrupt his thoughts or tasks, and mostly watched at first. It's possible that the intensity of my obvious observation earned answers to my questions, once asked. Most entrepreneurs appreciate precocious children, as they were probably similarly inquisitive themselves. Curiosity is a requirement for invention. Every new business is an invention of sorts, even if it's not the first in an industry.

It took a grain of courage to approach Mr. Spikes with a question. He could actually be quite demeaning, considering the number of people he called "stupid." His general disposition and stature, along with the number of signs he created for employees and others that began or ended with "Stupid," were regarded by many as intimidating. Inwardly, I looked upon his style as more of a dry comedic act. Instead of complaining about a lack of respect, as the successful Rodney Dangerfield did regularly in his stand-up acts, Mr. Spikes demanded respect. He deserved it, too.

He had only a limited education and lacked an impressive vocabulary, yet I admired him greatly. Starting with nothing, he eventually owned and operated several businesses. Nearly every valuable lesson or skill he conveyed to me can be applied to any business. The gas station served as something of an anchor or "home base" to his many other ventures, so it was possible to learn new things within a variety of subjects.

Over time, Mr. Spikes came to like and trust me. When I turned 14, they put me on payroll at $4.75 an hour. I worked there all through high school and the first two years of college, with increases in wages and responsibilities along the way.

Although Big Buck's was retail—a gas station and store—it also offered other services such as check cashing. Every business requires more than one lane of information, skill, and ability to operate. By allowing my nonstop questions, Mr. Spikes and his children who helped manage the store provided me quite an education in how much business owners handle behind the scenes. Information about everything from ordering, inventory, costs, mark-ups, overhead, payroll, insurance, various licenses, and more was shared with me until I understood how to handle each task.

Learning a little bit about everything required in any business is extremely valuable. The "little bits" of information become significant and lead to a level of proficiency. Eventually, it's possible to know almost everything about a given business. At that point, as a generalist, one becomes very competent and valuable to any enterprise. Generalists are more valuable than "experts." Experts know single lanes of information and procedures only, and often apply the term "expert" to themselves. I was gifted to have the opportunity to become a generalist, which sparked further curiosity and confidence toward all things worth doing in business and life.

While mostly part-time, I had become capable in every aspect of running the business and handled bits of everything as needed. Because we cashed people's payroll checks as a service, I could see what the area townspeople were earning. It was clear that keeping their families fed was not an easy task.

Many of the checks were those of heads of households. In no small way, this experience was something that motivated me. It strengthened my resolve to achieve financial security and independence. Both Mr. Spikes and my mother were terrific living examples of how to welcome hard work and jump any hurdle thrown in the way of progress and eventual success.

Mr. Spikes was probably responsible for supporting hundreds of families at some level over the years. In Southport, that's a good chunk of the area's population. He made his initial money running chicken farms, and then accumulated several properties to operate more chicken farms. As the gas station and convenience store business continued to grow to include additional gas stations and thus demand more and more of his attention, he would still go out every day to work on the residential developments he was building. I don't think he slept much or wasted a lot of time.

Throughout my adult life, I've retained the lessons I learned. Business basics are fundamental, like how to be mindful of expenses and that soft costs can get out of hand. He was a mentor without intending to be one. The lessons learned from my grandfather were echoed by Mr. Spikes in an industry far removed from electronics or mechanics: You can't fix anything unless you find the "why,"—the underlying reason the problem exists in the first place.

Exactly the same process is used by those serious about actually solving any problem—you must start by finding out what is causing the problem. To date, the only industry that fails to take that first step is government at every level. The layering of laws and regulations only exacerbates problems and pushes any solutions down the road. Sadly, some are pushed so far that they're beyond repair unless leaders muster the courage to take bold steps.

Aside from all the hard work, Mr. Spikes also managed to keep the town entertained in a funny sort of way. His contributions to entertainment were likely also not intended to be entertainment, but they remain legendary. Instead of trying to be everywhere at once to supervise all employees, he'd erect hand-made signs on plywood or carboard and post them everywhere. Each one began or ended with "Stupid!" Some memorable signs were directed toward not only employees, but anyone who attempted to do something stupid, such as, "Stupid! Don't dump your trash in my dumpsters!"

There were many such signs. Now that he's gone nearly five years, I'm probably not the only one who misses those little chuckles when passing through Southport today. His signs were so talked about (quietly, of course) that I almost think Big Buck's should consider selling tiny replicas of the best as souvenirs. The employee restroom, for example, would have a "Stupid! Wash your hands!" sign. And, if you were hauling empty boxes, you'd be reminded with, "Stupid! Don't just stack them up, break them down!"

If Mr. Spikes were still alive today, he'd likely pay anyone willing to drive to the steps of Congress to erect a sign: "Stupid! Stop Throwing Our Money at Problems! Find the "WHY" and Fix Them!" Or, one that he famously hung at Big Buck's and probably each of his other gas stations: "Thieves Get Shot!"

6

BEYOND THE DIRT ROADS

AFTER MY INITIAL SEVERAL years at Big Buck's and graduation from high school, it became time to wander further, test my skills, and develop more of them in preparation for full-fledged adulthood. Always a year ahead of other students my age, I was a young 17 years old and hardly an adult even though I felt like one after having received a diploma. I had no interest in sticking around, taking a year off, or in any delays to moving forward with what seemed my natural course.

I enrolled as an undergraduate at the University of West Florida in Pensacola and declared Electrical Engineering as my major course of study. Pensacola made sense to me because it was just two hours away from my family. I had no interest in competing with anyone from anywhere to attend a faraway big-name school with big price tags. My goal was to do what seemed a logical next step and keep moving forward.

After all, as Thomas Sowell famously suggested during an interview conducted by Peter Robinson, "You might say *the road to hell is paved* with Ivy League degrees."

Electrical engineering is some fairly straightforward stuff. Circuits either work or they don't, and if they don't, you fix them. It seemed illogical to me that a tuition several times what I'd pay to the University of West Florida, such as for M.I.T., would prepare me better in some way, or that the laws of electricity would be any different elsewhere. What seemed important to both life and electricity was to make sure everything stayed *grounded*.

Nothing was perfectly planned, aligned, in place, or even paid for when I decided it was time to move ahead. I did manage to buy a car at age 16 for $300 (because it didn't run), and then fixed it in our dusty driveway because we didn't have a garage. I also managed to total it within a year. It was a 1982 Mustang. That's not something most people would get too excited about unless they were just 16 years old and fixed it themselves. I was sure proud of that car.

Before the car was destroyed, I worked hard to keep it meticulously clean. Unfortunately, because we lived on a dirt road, when I took it out to show and share rides with area friends, it would be covered in dust before I made it to the end of our driveway. What was worse is that once the totaled vehicle was headed back to the graveyard where I'd rescued it from in the first place, I realized Pensacola really wasn't close enough to Southport! College start dates were not far off and I was now without a vehicle.

Parents in Southport didn't say things like, "You're about to turn 16. Let's find a car for you!" I'm aware that similar conversations take place in some families, but I'm convinced that it doesn't happen in most families in the United States, and that's a good thing! Parenting is about building independence and strength in children, not developing and encouraging dependency. My family did a good job of encouraging me to work for what I wanted and not to expect a handout from anyone.

That's another thing that government gets wrong. While I used to believe that our federal government truly cared about citizens and was dedicated to promoting life, liberty, and the pursuit of happiness, many within the halls of Congress today are hellbent on behavior control. To achieve that, they intentionally create dependency by throwing money and incentives to those who comply with their idea of utopia. America, the 'great melting pot,' was forged not to harness the hearts, minds, and souls of its citizens, but rather to achieve the opposite. The purpose of America is to create an environment where freedom rings!

The conditions necessary for freedom require that people also have the right to be wrong, the right to make mistakes, and the right to make decisions about their own lives. It's personal responsibility that strengthens civil society, not a top down "nanny state." Those who wish to control people, redistribute wealth, and pick winners and losers, do not trust citizens. They've got the entire structure of this republic upside down. The question should be, 'what can our statesmen do to maintain our trust in government?' Give the people information and let them choose what they think is best.

After some weeks of financial recovery, I managed to pull together enough to buy a 1993 Ford Probe. That car got me to Pensacola and gave me a wee bit of bragging rights as it was *under* ten years old in 2001. At the time, the car was amazing to me, and I could get to where I needed to be, until its engine threw a rod and failed. That was all the more reason for me to concentrate fully on studies and get the job done.

While I did eventually acquire a new upgrade in wheels—a Mitsubishi Eclipse—with the help of my grandfather who co-signed a loan to help me get into something that would last more than a year, my interest in engineering as a course of study started to wane. Of course, I made all the car payments, so my grandfather never had a worry, but I was eager to get back to work, back to business, and back to making money instead of spending it. Textbook versions of what I'd already learned hands-on from my grandfather were dull, to say the least.

At a minimum, I'd certainly have to change my major in order to branch out into new areas of study. Still, all I could think about was starting my own business, and I couldn't settle on any other major that would hold my attention for very long. I really felt I was largely sitting idle, and I could see the money, my *own* hard-earned money, flying out the window. So, after two years, I dropped out.

Many business leaders will tell you that real education happens outside of classrooms. Had I been in school on a government handout, I may not have made the right choice. A fast track through the process of education was important to me. I wanted to get out there and start a business, or even many businesses, and actually ride that roller coaster of life adults had always warned us about.

That's when I realized it was true—real learning happens when you grab the wheel of life, engage, and make decisions, whether good or bad. The trick is to make more good decisions than bad. Consequences matter, and if you have a free ride, they largely disappear until it's too late to regain independence and rational thought. What is lost is the very thing that feeds the hearts and souls of men—freedom.

Before actually cutting the cord, I'd done some research. I initially wanted to buy a gas station, but I didn't have quite enough money and couldn't secure a loan. It didn't much matter what type of business I would someday own, but rather that I would own it and could see a path toward profitability. I searched for distressed businesses and businesses that were for sale. At this point, it didn't really matter where it was either, as long as I could make it work.

Oddly enough, I initially settled on a custom chocolate manufacturing and retail company in San Francisco. It produced things such as business cards, branded party favors, corporate logos, and other attention getters—all made out of chocolate. Why should a business put out grocery store candy to lure visitors to their tradeshow booth when they could hand out their custom chocolate logo in a variety of colors and flavors?

The business was being offered for what I thought was a steal. I hopped a flight to the city by the Bay, bought the chocolate factory, and began the work of systemizing the existing businesses to make it more efficient. The place turned around in no time, employees kept their jobs, and the books moved from red to black ink. Though with the costs of living in San Francisco, even back then, it was never enough.

Many businesses are great concepts, but they're inefficient because well-intentioned founders haven't adequately considered the development of procedures, through research or experimentation, in order to produce cost effective and consistent operations. Many problems a business encounters will likely be seen repeatedly unless a complete correction can be applied, or a uniform procedure to cure the problem is in place. Customer service is a great example of where issues are seen repeatedly—a lost shipment, damaged product, wrong order, etc. As long as people remain imperfect, so will businesses. Policies are required so that all customer service issues are handled gracefully, efficiently, uniformly, and fairly, without metaphorically selling the farm.

So, while almost every entrepreneur is hard working from morning to night, 7 days per week, many start-ups run capital deficits, show little to no profit, and ultimately fail. Meanwhile, the owners who tried their best are often ready to drop dead from exhaustion. Entrepreneurs are characteristically optimistic. While that's refreshing and necessary, it also means that too many start-ups anticipate things will always go as planned. It's a bit like a football coach imagining that people will move along the field exactly as he draws the "X's" and "0's" on a chalkboard in the locker room.

Many business owners throw their arms up in frustration after repeated blows. At that point, their choice is to hire experts to help or sell. If money is the problem, they have no choice unless a consultant or expert is willing to work for deferred payment—a risk few professionals would take. This doesn't mean the business concept was poor. It may simply mean that systems needed to be developed or reconfigured to forge a path toward success.

Optimizing and systematizing struggling businesses turned out to be something I had a natural ability to do. I found I could identify the root problem and then try different solutions until I found the right one. I like to recall Edison's thousands of attempts prior to finding a workable filament for the electric light bulb. Had he stopped after the first few thousand failures, we may still be reading by candlelight. Perseverance, faith, and a logical series of actions lead to progress. I like solving problems and knowing that I left something better than I found it.

This touches heavily on another area in which government is out of sync with common sense. Most government programs fail, and when they do, too often more money is thrown at the failed initiatives. It's fake money. It's borrowed money. It's money we don't have, and at this point, money we cannot recover or repay. It's driving up inflation and devaluing the hard-earned savings of everyday Americans, all to prop up failure.

So, year after year, taxpayers are forced to watch a circus in which they are not allowed to participate beyond the role of spectator. What they see are failed programs posting bigger losses, year in and year out, on their dime.

Instead of asking for expertise, ending an admittedly failed initiative, or resigning from office to let a qualified individual take the reins, politicians ask for more money to fuel these failed programs and beg for an opportunity to be re-elected so they can fix the problem they've already failed to fix after years of trying.

It really doesn't matter what kind of heartwarming name a program or initiative has—and they all have them (e.g., The *Care* Act)—to suggest you're heartless unless you support it. Citizens see right through this nonsense but are cut out from most opportunities to do anything about it beyond contacting their representatives. What's also true is that every program carries a hefty price tag, and what remains unchecked and little understood by the public is how much the government pays itself to administer those failing programs. The endless reporting upon reporting, the reviews of reviews, and the number of people apparently required to administer funding and make sure grantees or contractors are doing their jobs would make your head spin.

I met with a State Attorney recently who explained that while he needed more prosecutors, and there was a federal grant he could seek to cover two new prosecutors, it would take two or three people's efforts to maintain the level of documentation and communication required by the grant administrator, and thus wasn't practical for him to receive the grant at all. That is common—programs are put into place to look good but often don't do much good. They waste taxpayer dollars and provide a talking point for the sponsor of the bill as they seek re-election to another term of saying much and accomplishing little.

It's disappointingly common for the cumulative administrative costs of a contract or grant to exceed the amount of the contract or grant itself. They are budgeted and accounted for differently, and to learn the total costs of any particular program or agreement, ordinary citizens would need to dig through bureaucratic agencies and various systems of recording and accounting.

You've likely heard the phrase, "lies, damned lies, and statistics," which implies that statistics are more dishonest than both "lies" and "damned lies." We need to add "government statistics" to that line because the only thing more misleading than statistics are government statistics. Only government would shut down businesses nationally by mandates, ensuring the loss of millions of jobs, then once the emergency mandates expire, claim the people who return back to their jobs are "government created jobs." These government shutdowns were unconstitutional and repugnant to a free society, but that is for another chapter.

If any business operated in the same manner as our government, they wouldn't last six months. At least most private business owners are honest. If they see a looming train wreck ahead or are in over their heads, they ask for help or sell their business. Nobody is coming to their rescue, nor should they. The freedom to make potentially wrong decisions should be coupled with the individual responsibility for those decisions. Bailouts that remove the consequences for our decisions render the decisions made by individuals irrelevant.

The same should be true for businesses deemed "too big to fail," and government programs that show little to no efficacy. The "too big to fail" companies can hardly be regarded as "private" once they've devoured trillions of taxpayer dollars in the form of bailouts. Bailouts enable bad behavior. Most people don't "bailout" their kids, at least not without strings attached, and certainly not with other people's money. That's a surefire way to create monsters.

Overall, the custom chocolate company was fun, and San Francisco was still beautiful back then. Being able to adapt to California culture from Florida's panhandle region was a hoot, but I managed. I worked to keep my eyes in their sockets upon experiencing the cost of living and obvious amounts of disposable income deployed toward making impressions upon others with style, flair, clothing, wealth, or whatever else one wanted to flaunt. Much of it seemed inauthentic, but it was entertaining, nonetheless.

There was also the complete opposite end of the economic spectrum on display in the same city—homelessness, desperation, and decay. Nobody seemed to know their neighbors, or at least not many of them. To "know" a neighbor seemed to mean that you could simply remember and recite their name. Everybody seemed to be living in their own world.

I often wondered how those flaunting whatever they deemed extraordinary about themselves managed to walk past so many living a completely different and obviously difficult life. Not that anyone could stop to help or would even know how to help. But it was odd that some carried on as though they never even saw the people they pointedly avoided while walking though parks and on sidewalks.

My task was to turn the chocolate company around, and I did. Mostly, it was done by improving systems of management. I eventually saw profit and expected to see more. It was a successful exercise. However, I couldn't see past one location. It was such a niche business that a franchise or multiple locations seemed unworkable. There was no viable opportunity for expansion. It was a business for somebody who loved customized marketing and related services, loved chocolate, and loved San Francisco.

I knew San Francisco wasn't for me when at least once per month I'd have someone stop in the shop and suggest that I take down my American Flag that was hanging out front, claiming it was offensive and nationalistic. At the time, we were in the midst of the second Gulf War and people in San Francisco seemed more interested in appeasing foreign threats than in protecting our homeland.

After turning the business upright, I knew it wasn't for me over the long haul. I wanted to get back to the Southeast. The chocolate company sold at a profit and I set out to locate a new business.

7

MEAT AND POTATOES
IN AMERICA

MY NEXT SEARCH FOR a business to acquire turned up a steak house in Gaithersburg, Maryland. This came about as I looked online for businesses listed for sale. With each possibility, I'd have to find answers to questions like, "How much are they asking," "What does it earn," and, "How will I pay for it?" These were the same questions I sought answers to when previously settling on the custom chocolate company. I was hoping to find something that I could afford and which would pay for itself in just a few years.

Restaurants are extremely risky. Yet, I did have experience working in them. As a busboy at popular beach front joints during tourist season in Panama City, I watched what every employee did and learned from them. I was far from an expert, but I certainly had an understanding of how to run a restaurant. Much of it is common sense to those who have ever eaten in restaurants with a mind toward what must happen behind the scenes. Everyone, of course, knows what they expect when dining out. So, to figure out what is required to make that happen isn't any great stretch.

A move to operating a steakhouse would get me closer to the South. While some consider Maryland to be South, it's not quite where I imagine South to be, but it certainly is East of San Francisco and was a step in the right direction for me. I had no particular affinity for Maryland, but I'd take a good deal wherever I found it. Before leaving the University of West Florida, I'd already purchased a house at age 18 and had been renting it out. I'd saved up as much as I could along the way and had what I thought was more than enough security for me to take another leap, and so I did.

As is common for a business in distress, the steakhouse books were a mess, so I acquired the place at a very good price. It was a business where the owner had clearly been out of the picture for several months and it needed on-site management. It didn't take long to straighten things out, systematize operations, and start seeing better returns. But, as life would have it, two unexpected things got in the way. One was that while I never thought I would get sick of steak and potatoes, I did!

Steaks are easy to prepare, and most Americans love them. While there were other choices on the menu, mostly all customers would order steak. Steak and fries, steak and fries—all night, every night. There was nothing new happening in the kitchen or any part of the operation because people came there for one thing only—the menu they'd enjoyed for decades in this well-established steak house. The task was to make sure the steaks were properly prepared and consistently satisfying while also turning a profit.

I started to smell like steak, and so did everything I owned. It was inescapable. My hair, pillow, couch, car, and blue jeans all smelled like steak and fries. It's not that I don't enjoy a good steak and fries myself or am offended by the smell. It's rather that I'd like just my meal to carry that nice aroma—the same experience as the customers enjoyed. Instead, I carried the smell wherever I went throughout the day. Even a hot shower couldn't erase the scent of what I'd rather eat than smell every minute. It's hard to avoid. The kitchen is hot, and smoke really does get in your eyes—and everything else.

Few likely noticed that I constantly smelled like meat and potatoes because, as any restaurateur will tell you, owners seldom wander off the trail connecting home and work. There's simply no time. That's why the goal is a chain of restaurants with various cuisines and group branding, or a franchise. While this restaurant by the name of "Chris' Steakhouse" (after its Greek founder) was now in the black, it was never going to rise up and contend with "Ruth's Chris Steakhouse" and that group's locations, which now line the east coast and beyond with over 100 restaurants.

Part of the reason for this inevitable outcome was the timing. With the economic downturn which began in 2006, many found themselves out of work and on unemployment assistance. "Free" money always hurts the hospitality industry because, while many pick up hours when they can for extra cash despite being otherwise more gainfully employed full-time, government assistance feels more like a long-term paid vacation so they don't seek extra hours. In fact, the government assistance makes it impossible for those who might like to earn extra money on the side, because they would then lose that benefit which is, under the lawful conditions of receiving assistance, the "meat and potatoes" of their existence until economic conditions improve.

It was so difficult to find and keep employees that I worked all day, every day, and sometimes found it necessary to sleep a few hours curled up in one of the booths at the restaurant instead of losing precious time traveling home late at night only to return in the morning. Sometimes, staff simply didn't show up and I'd end up doing dishes, restocking, and resetting tables until I was simply too tired to drive home.

After a few years, I decided to hunt down a new opportunity, with an eye toward a restaurant that would serve lighter and healthier food. I didn't find one matching the concept I had in mind, but I did find what seemed to be a good location for a new restaurant across from Emory University in Atlanta.

My mind went to work immediately developing the concept I called "Sprouts." I sold the steakhouse, moved to Atlanta to develop my concept for what became "Sprouts Green Café," and took some time off for planning—this time with a nice profit from the sale of my steakhouse in the bank.

At long last, I was back in the real South, and happily, rather close to Florida. Back to Southern hospitality, Southern cooking, and Southern style. Back to manners and common courtesies such as "please," "thank you," "you're welcome," "sir," "ma'am," and even, "no, you go first, really, please go ahead of me."

You can really recognize somebody who was raised in the South by their manners, which are sewn into their souls, and I'm glad for it. Life is too short to be unkind to others, and great manners make life more beautiful for everyone. That doesn't mean anyone needs to be a doormat; it just means that a show of respect for others and knowing how to do that is important in a civilized society (which seems to be endangered today).

Being from the South is not a requirement for being polite, showing good manners, or respecting others. Maybe that's the thing—we Southerners should let others know that we don't hold a patent on civility. Everyone is welcome and invited to compete!

A current search for best restaurants in Gaithersburg today pulls up a list from 1—625, so I'm glad I no longer own one of them. Back then, in about 2008, my stock portfolio was hemorrhaging (as was everyone else's) so I set up the test site for Sprouts Green Cafe with an eye towards potentially franchising the concept once it was proven.

Let the southern downpours, monsoons, and steam fast-track the growth of Sprouts, and yet another new venture, I prayed!

8

LEANER MENU, LEANER MARGINS

I TOOK A BREATHER for nearly two years once in Atlanta. Places were popping up constantly, and more and more establishments failed in the great recession that occurred from late 2007—2009. Restaurants are risky enough, so I felt no rush to increase that risk during a period of marked economic decline. Meanwhile, I gave thought to a new concept and what would likely be very different clientele given the University location I was considering.

Menu items that would cater to college students had to be quick, varied, and relatively inexpensive. Trends toward healthier choices and unusual foods continued to emerge. Ethnic foods seemed to be all the rage as eating things you've never heard of became increasingly popular. Those who would likely have turned up their noses at raw fish were eating sushi, and suddenly kale was in salads. It was important to pretend to be a "foodie" even if you weren't one, and to know how to pronounce "quinoa" to keep up with popular conversations.

Emory, a private research university located in the Northeast quadrant of downtown Atlanta, has a relatively small student population with a total enrollment of under 15,000. Tuition, however, is pricey and it's not an easy admissions establishment. So, students there aren't stupid or poor, and every college campus the world over has a myriad of eateries within walking distance.

I decided to be trendy, but not over the top exotic for fear it would add risk. Besides, I don't know exotic foods. Aside from a greater number of ingredients with relatively short shelf lives to order, I did think the new restaurant had potential for a franchise. So many successful food stops seemed to have outlets near several universities. I could imagine Sprouts fitting in with the rest. Anticipating the travel that would eventually be required, I bought an airplane and learned to fly it.

It's not that I was an avid fan of aviation, but again, it was just a matter of practicality. With the plane, I could also get back to Panama City to visit my family in a little over an hour instead of six hours of driving. Owning a restaurant, especially a start-up with a single location, really means being able to live there and hopefully being able to escape for a few hours each night in order to sleep in a real bed. Customers see the "open" hours posted on a door or window. They don't see the hours required for operation, which would likely read "almost all of them."

Once opened, our turkey panini proved popular. It's one of those items that straddles the fence between hip and ordinary because it's not a turkey sandwich. A turkey sandwich would have sold less well to college students—that's what their grandparents eat. Avocado toast became trendy about then, as did rice bowls with fresh vegetables, so we served those too, along with fresh juices and smoothies.

Each of the healthier choice items presented in a new way sold better than guacamole, fried rice, and shakes probably would have.

Sometimes trends in eateries are just a matter of how many languages are inserted into menu descriptions. It's a bit like writing wine descriptions and dropping the word "chocolate" as a prominent and promised bouquet. Nearly every industry plays the language game. How else would furniture stores be able to offer an "espresso" couch?

I always got a kick out of customers who asked questions only to learn that the colorful description on the menu is just a foreign language word for something they've eaten routinely and have recognized by its English name for all of their lives. They asked, and they deserved an honest answer—'that's right, a scallion is a kind of a midget onion. It's just an onion.' The rest of the game is sell, sell, sell!

Word games should be banned from use by government, but they're not. Congress deploys similar tactics when pitching spending bills. Their descriptions, however, require English to English translation, and descriptive phrases often mean the exact opposite of what any sound reader may interpret upon first glance. They're intentionally deceptive. Scroll through the Congressional Record to quickly pick up on some of the utter nonsense and misleading phrases.

It's not okay for Congress to play word games with the American people while spending taxpayer's dollars to boot. But I think it's fine for a restaurant to play the language game. Dining out is an experience on many levels. Creativity is part of the art of being a restaurateur, and customers playing by paying is optional. It's not actually deceptive. It's creative. If you know other cuisines, multiple language descriptions are actually more precise than English versions of similar ingredients or components of a menu item.

"Panini," for example, is an Italian bread of a certain shape and density. The actual English translation would be "bun." Most Americans would assume that to be a hamburger bun or hard roll, but Panini really is something a bit different. It's not that it's anything truly different than a bun, but that it's shaped to be sliced horizontally, and is more thin and dense than what Americans might think of as a bun, intended to hold a single serving of sandwich, unlike an airy slice from any loaf of bread.

So, anyone who thinks panini is healthier than a slice of bread is sadly mistaken. But it sounds good, it's "cool" compared to the sandwich your grandparents ate, it tastes delicious, and that means it sells.

Trends are risky because they're trendy. They are moving targets. They're here today, gone tomorrow. Many people don't really want what the trends pressure them into thinking they want. But unsuspecting, late-maturing individuals get lured into a world of make believe in order to appear to be hip or popular.

If a college student went to lunch with several new friends and requested a turkey sandwich over a "Panini," there's a very great risk that the new friends might conclude the sandwich lover is away from home for the very first time. Sandwich lovers are not "cool."

However, there is very great value in classic traditions. They hold value because they've withstood the test of time. That's how they became classics. This is true of everything we value in life and cultures around the globe. And honesty is often a breath of fresh air, or music to one's ears. It's the reason for the famous line of a child who blurts out, "the emperor wears no clothes," in the popular fable passed down for centuries, most famously by the Greek storyteller Aesop, and later in Hans Christian Anderson's "The Emperor's New Clothes."

Getting my new, healthier restaurant up and running was quickly made memorable when a woman walked in asking for ice cream. I explained that we didn't have any ice cream, but I could offer her some yogurt.

She replied, "No baby, no baby, there ain't enough fat in that!"

It wasn't long after that when I came to the realization that there wasn't enough fat in the margins of a single healthy food restaurant, either. Around the same time, in 2009, I met my life partner, Scott Marr. We bonded instantly over our mutual love for business and innovation. At that time, he was just getting started with a business of his own called Fleet Clean USA, a truck washing company.

After days and weeks of discussing next steps, I came to the conclusion that Sprouts really didn't hold the profit margins required to launch a successful franchise, and we teamed up to push Fleet Clean forward and build it into a national brand.

Keith Gross celebrating his 4ᵗʰ birthday.

*Keith Gross Halloween 1987
in Bay County Florida.*

Young, Keith Gross pictured with his pet dog, Scooter

Young, Keith Gross behind the plate,
Bay County Little League

Keith Gross High School graduation.

Keith Gross pictured along side mother, Rhonda shortly after obtaining his pilot's license.

Keith Gross pictured during active duty with the National Guard.

Keith Gross with husband and business partner, Scott Marr.

Keith Gross, 2024 US Senate Campaign official headshot.

Keith Gross chats with Vietnam war vet in Central Florida Veteran's Day 2023

Keith Gross outside of Florida vs Florida State rivalry game during his 2023 Football and Freedom tour.

Keith Gross on the campaign trail in Chattahoochee, Fl January 2024

Keith Gross rallies the crowd during a Walton County bus stop as part of his 2024 US Senate campaign.

9

CAMPING FOR CLIENTS

SPROUTS SOLD IN 2010, again with a healthy profit from my two years of developing the restaurant. While still in Atlanta, I decided to enroll in Florida State University to finish my undergraduate degree. The task now was to build market share for Fleet Clean while also completing course work remotely. That meant a considerable amount of travel along with many early mornings and late nights.

We lived in an RV trailer while travelling the country to build new locations for Fleet Clean. This wasn't the fun, adventure-filled type of camping I enjoyed in my youth. This was simply a practical way to save money while building out new locations and calling on potential new customers.

Fleet Clean's competitive advantage was that we built special trucks which would carry all of the water needed for the job instead of hooking up to a client's utilities. We often stayed overnight in the parking lots of our business locations to save hotel fees and be on the spot, ready for work. Our largest competitor was a company called "Fleet Wash," and we were quickly gaining on them because of the amount of flexibility we had created through the use of our specialized equipment and good customer service. Often, vendors in this industry would promise to show up and then fail to deliver. That kind of failure might result in cancelled truckloads of food if the trailer wasn't cleaned out on time. We believe in saying what you mean and meaning what you say, and we developed a reputation for reliability, accuracy, and integrity in a field where these qualities were uncommon.

We reclaimed the water used, and our trucks could carry 1025 gallons while the competition would often show up with 100 gallons of water and expect to hook up on site. Our company grew from having a single location to dozens of offices from Miami to Seattle. When building out new locations, we'd take the RV and live in it for months while hiring and training new employees, in order to greatly reduce overhead costs.

It was necessary to hire and train long before we actually needed employees because of the fast growth. It was also important for me to schedule about twice as many employees as were actually needed because even though we paid well, half of them wouldn't show up for the job. The work is strenuous—we hand-brushed each truck—and there's nothing pleasant about filthy trucks. That worked in our favor, however, because nobody really wants to wash trucks and companies were desperate for vendors. The only obstacles to even faster growth were the number of hours in a day and how quickly we could train crews.

In relatively little time, Fleet Clean became the second largest truck washing company in the country, with Fleet Wash in the number one position. With several successful locations, we put together a franchise opportunity that also grew quickly. At the top of our game, we had more than 50 direct hire employees, hundreds of others when counting the franchises, and no shortage of clientele. Some of our biggest clients did our sales and new market development for us by asking us to set up locations near their multiple operations. Once established in a new market with a few of our large regular clients, we'd work to form relationships with other smaller or regional companies in the area. We were taking market share from the larger players every month.

In the beginning of this endeavor, banks had declined our applications for loans to grow what quickly became a wildly successful business. While it was disappointing at the time, in retrospect I'm very happy banks declined our applications for loans. Lines of credit really may have destroyed our ability to pull ahead financially. Everything we made went straight back into the company to fuel growth, and we were forced to be extremely judicious about how we spent money. We were perpetually motivated to make every single initiative successful in order to generate maximum profit, and carefully accounted for every dollar being spent. It was often a juggling match because all our costs were paid up front— water, supplies, travel, trucks, time, and payroll. The payments from our customers usually didn't arrive until a month or two after the jobs were finished. most were on a recurring service schedule. So, we could budget expenses, but cash was consistently tight.

Nearly every business owner will tell you that not every account pays on time, and every once in a while, owners get stiffed by some nonpaying client. Still, I'm happy we handled operations without the help of substantial loans. That's a major problem we suffer at the hands of our government. Whenever they want to spend, they raise the debt ceiling, print more money, and fatten programs to their delight with some false idea that they are "helping" Americans.

Our national debt is absolutely out of control and virtually nothing seems to ever get fixed or solved. Failing programs never end. There's no "mission accomplished." Not receiving lines of credit for Fleet Clean allowed me to face problems head on and fix them. At the time, there were no models or financials banks could use to provide loans, and I think it is one of the greatest blessings we ever received while building out Fleet Clean. We were forced to ensure profitable operations because we were operating without a safety net. There were weeks when we had to use credit card cash advances to make payroll, not because we were unprofitable but because all of our money was sitting on our books as Accounts Receivable; money customers owed us but hadn't paid yet. Employees needed to be paid reliably every week, so we sacrificed and took up the slack personally to ensure our business continued to move forward.

Things were moving quickly and with plenty of beautiful scenery to enjoy as we traversed nearly the entire country. My boxer, Angel, kept us company and at one point we had a baby owl show up on our doorstep. Not knowing exactly how to care for an owl, we fed it chicken, beef, or whatever we were cooking until it flew away a few days later. One uncertainty was internet access along the way while taking online courses, but in 2014 I received my bachelor's degree in public safety and law enforcement intelligence.

Moving about in an RV really provides an opportunity to appreciate the tremendous beauty and size of the United States. While traveling, we developed models not only for the Fleet Clean business, but for other franchises that we could launch, operate, and sell. As a matter of practicality, I enrolled at the University of Montana School of Law to pursue a degree. Lawyers are expensive, and with all of the contracts and agreements I was drafting and negotiating, I could just be one myself.

That's why Scott is the CEO and I'm the "strategist." Besides, I didn't want to get sold with one of our companies when we would eventually sell, which often happens to C-suite execs when the buyer wants to maintain continuity of business. No, no, no, not for me. I want to sell and then move on to the next venture.

And I'll let you in on a little secret: I just show up at the meetings without announcing I'm General

Counsel for our companies. The reason is that once another company knows you are bringing your lawyer to a meeting, they feel compelled to have their attorney participate too. That's when things become complicated, drawn out, and more expensive than they need to be.

Once settled in Missoula, Montana in order to attend law school (yes, you have to be there), I also joined the Montana Army National Guard. I felt compelled to do what I could as then, many of our U.S. soldiers were facing conflict in the Middle East. My family had a long record of service and I enlisted as an intelligence analyst.

10

GOD AND NATURE
IN MONTANA

IT WASN'T FLORIDA, BUT Montana was interesting and beautiful, albeit often a bit chilly. During any spare time, I'd head to the mountains to walk, bike, or ski some trails. There were streams to paddle and fish to catch, and there was time to contemplate God and the world while admiring all of His creations. Although I don't attend any church regularly today, my faith in God has always been a significant part of my being.

I started my education in a private Christian elementary school and continued there until the third grade when my family just couldn't afford it any longer. In fact, my mother was a Sunday school teacher at the church we attended, and sometimes classes would convene in our home instead of at the church. We were in church every Wednesday and every Sunday for many years. It was also common for us to go to church on other days for worship or various other community functions.

Back in Southport, we lived on "New Church Road." We helped to take care of the new church by riding a lawnmower down the block to cut the grass there. Many of my friends belonged to our church. It may be particularly true of rural areas, but our congregation was something of an extended family. Everybody knew everybody else. Getting together to celebrate our faith was both a social and spiritual event. Knowing your faith is shared by others you care about strengthens a community and reminds us that there is something greater than ourselves.

Missoula, Montana is surrounded by nature. There were national forests and parks in every direction from our home. The campus itself was a short distance away on foot. Similar to Florida's panhandle region, it was heavily populated with wildlife, some of them dangerous, but all of them majestic, nonetheless. It was a fascinating new chapter in my adult life, and one that only increased my love for our great country.

Scott routinely travelled to Florida to handle day-to-day operations in what became our head-quarters in Melbourne. We didn't actually choose Melbourne, it chose us, primarily because of a key employee operating from there. For many years she was the glue that kept things together. A short number of years later, we'd all come to live in the same city, along with other key employees, for efficiency.

Meanwhile, I was busy studying law and negotiating contracts for Fleet Clean, with several trips to and from Florida and other locations as required. I remember many weekends when I had to go train a new manager or help solve a problem at one of our locations, and still get back on time for classes the next week.

Having a plane was always a tool for saving time. My first plane was a 1960 Mooney—a single engine, piston-driven craft that was relatively fast and fuel efficient. If that type of engine fails, you're going down, and the outcome is often just a matter of how far you can glide. Hopefully, a safe field is within gliding distance. It was a time saver and it was what I could afford at the time.

Readily negotiating fluctuations in air temperatures, altitudes, and winds in mountain air became an obvious necessity. While I upgraded wings along the way, I wasn't able to make the jump to a truly better plane overnight. My second plane was just a newer version of my first, also a Mooney. Engine failure in that plane nearly brought my own life, as well as Scott's and two additional passengers, to a premature end.

While flying over the Okefenokee Swamp in Florida, I could hear the engine sputter and knew we were losing altitude. It had no auto pilot and no GPS. I was flying the plane by hand. We had a paper map but they're huge—4'x3'—opened by section. I switched off the intercoms to the napping backseat passengers so they wouldn't be alarmed by conversations taking place in the cockpit, and asked Scott where we were on the map—what was the nearest airport?

"Oh, I already folded that up and put it away," he answered. We were just below the clouds at 6,000—7,000 feet and Scott was getting motion sickness.

Well, okay, I thought, trying to remain calm. So, we pulled the map back out and found the nearest airport as best we could. You can't really know exactly where you are without more advanced navigation technology. Thankfully, airplanes can glide a fairly long distance to a safe landing in most cases, so the trick was to stay calm and find someplace to land.

On this plane, I had an airport directory; a green book that looks a lot like a small phonebook. I had to comb through the thing, then look up the radio frequency of what I thought was the nearest airport, dial it in, and hope for the best. Each airport has three frequencies—pilots, control tower, and ground.

It seemed I was closest to Lake City Airport. I dialed in the frequency for the control tower. No answer. I tried again, and again. Then, I switched to what might better get somebody's attention: "Mayday! Mayday! Mayday!"

Nothing came back beyond the usual eerie crackle of an old radio dwarfed by the loud banging of a dying engine that sputtered to life and died again about every thirty seconds.

Eventually a runway was in sight and despite never hearing back from anyone on the radio, I landed anyway. The engine was still spitting the sounds of a disorganized rifle range, and we didn't make it off the runway. An old man came hobbling out of a hanger. Herb was a WWII aircraft mechanic.

"Y'all seem to be having some trouble," he said.

Considering I had just landed on a runway without clearance and I could see a control tower, I fully expected an irate controller to greet me. Perhaps I had been radioing the wrong tower and perhaps I had landed somewhere other than Lake City. Its not like there are exit signs as you turn in for the final approach, so if you're not sure where you are, you probably will not be sure until after you've landed.

After confirming we were indeed at Lake City Airport, Herb explained, "Oh, yeah, tower's closed on the weekends here." He owned a maintenance shop so he was there working on a Sunday, and he helped us get the plane off of the runway and over to his hangar.

Herb was kind enough to take a look at the aircraft. He said the engine was almost falling off completely. It was tilting downward. Automotive grade lock washers were used by a previous "mechanic." The washers had plastic innards, which melted.

Ordinarily, a plane can glide to land in a field, a country road, or someplace nearby because it's balanced. If the engine falls off, a plane will go tail down, and you're dead. You'll have no warning and will be just minutes away from becoming a lawn dart. We were lucky to be alive. I wanted to kiss the ground.

We cancelled our trip to Miami, rented a car, and drove to Panama City to be with my family. Some experiences in life just make you appreciate life a whole lot more.

As is true about anything worth doing in life, you can't give up just because things are difficult. Flying was still an important advantage to have for the business. It saves oodles of time, and time is money. So, I vowed to get pre-purchase inspections. My next plane was a 1976 Piper Cherokee. It was a step up as it was *much* newer than the last plane, but it was terribly slow. I felt as though I could get outside and flap my arms faster than the plane could fly. In headwinds going out west, sometimes I was only tracking about 50 MPH over the ground.

Businesses always strive for greater efficiency and lower costs. I'm now on my fifth plane, because as you move to newer designs, they become bigger, faster, and safer. The reason I bought a plane and learned to fly in the first place was to make our business more efficient. Don't let the jetsetters with paid pilots, crew, and shared time subscriptions fool you. There's a stark difference between actions taken for efficiency and those taken for appearances.

I've always looked for practical, efficient solutions to business problems. In one of our businesses, we sold specially equipped trailers and struggled to source enough bare trailers to upfit. We tried every manufacturer in the country and couldn't get them to take our orders and deliver trailers in a timely fashion. We ended up establishing a trailer manufacturing company because our employees needed trailers to provide our services and we couldn't wait for the other manufacturers to clear their backlogs and eventually build what we needed. As the adage goes: if you want it done right, do it yourself.

Every time we hit a wall, we found or invented a solution. With a shorter lead time, it was less expensive to build and use our own. It's not hard to calculate what makes sense for business. Government should operate like a business, yet it is the only industry that, each year, whines about greater costs only to beg higher taxes from citizens, while showing less efficiency, if any.

Wouldn't it be nice if our elected officials and government learned to be more efficient over time? What explains how Government becomes more and more expensive each year, while the cost of nearly every technology in the private sector is reduced over time? Businesses are constantly reducing the cost of operations to increase their profit margins—so they can pay people and support more families. Businesses also strive to find more efficient ways to provide better service. Government seems to provide poor service consistently, without much attempt to improve the quality of service or reduce costs to citizens.

The only thing the government really produces is more regulations. Why should regulations cost anything in the first place? They are words on paper which provide officials tools to impose fines, charge fees, and even confiscate property. This nonsense confounds all citizens!

In 2015, while still in law school, Scott Marr and I upgraded our partnership . I married not only my best friend but also the greatest business partner I could have ever hoped for. We were dedicated to each other and to the success of our numerous endeavors, and continue to be thus dedicated to this day.

My current plane is a Phenom 100 by Embraer. While Embraer is a Brazilian company, its aircraft are assembled in Melbourne, Florida. After spending a few years living on Big Pine Key, (which often felt further from our home office than Montana) we decided to make it our home, much closer to our Melbourne company headquarters.

11

HEADING HOME

AT LONG LAST I was heading back to Florida. I received an administrative discharge from the Army National Guard in 2016 because of my pending move and the fact that deployments abroad were winding down. I would have also required retraining in Florida and that didn't seem logical to my superiors. I received my law degree in 2017, and that same year we bought a home on Big Pine Key in Florida and moved back to my home state.

It felt wonderful to be back in the real south, but we kept the house in Montana for periodic trips back to the mountains because we enjoyed that area so much. Hurricane Irma did some real damage to the property we purchased and restored on Big Pine Key. The "middle keys"—with Big Pine smack in the middle—were hardest hit by Irma.

As you might imagine, the cost of property restoration can be several times the price of purchase for wind torn structures, but there is great joy in being part of the solution and helping a community recover. The fear of impending hurricanes is something most coast dwellers have learned to manage. Generally, there is enough warning, along with estimations of paths and strengths of storms, that residents and emergency response teams know what is required to prepare for various tropical storms.

Waking up to or returning to see the damage is what rips the hearts out of individuals, families, and communities. Some lose absolutely everything, and much of what is lost cannot be replaced, such as family photos and keepsakes. When all is said and done, it's more painful to lose a family pet or photo album than to see the roof ripped from the top of your home, or what once was a beautiful grove of palm trees leveled to the ground.

Some people lose loved ones, too. Heartbreaking cases are of those who had no means to seek safer locations or even to communicate in order to request help. Equally heartbreaking are stories of emergency personnel or good Samaritans who lost their lives while trying to rescue others, and that's bound to happen every time because of the good nature—*the better angels of our nature*—inherent to most human beings. 133 people lost their lives in Irma alone.

Floridians are resilient. They're accustomed to preparing, rebuilding, and helping others. We were in a position to help by buying damaged property and working to quickly restore the waterfront, palm trees, roadways, and walkways. When mature palm trees are hauled in—hundreds of them—and planted quickly, their glorious fans hover high enough to be seen from a mile away in a flattened Florida, which is flat to begin with. The entire state holds an average elevation of 100 feet above sea level.

On Big Pine, homes are planted on a piece of protruding coral covered in sand, sitting at just three feet above sea level. We're just an extension of the beach.

Our property was a 3.5-acre area that we were able to bring back to life while providing jobs for many who needed income at the time. The home was also restored to well beyond its original beauty, inside and out. Investment by those able to do it is very much a way to give back to communities. Giving back to any community strengthens the whole of a state and country.

Aside from our modest effort, contributions pour in from people throughout Florida and the entire United States following most hurricanes. Volunteers arrive with trucks, equipment, food, clothing, skilled labor, and more. Everyone pitches in to restore what's needed so that citizens can return to a life with balance, opportunity, productivity, tranquility, and freedom. It is heartwarming, inspirational, and appreciated by everyone.

Catastrophic photos appear in many newsfeeds following hurricanes. Almost everyone knows somebody who resides either part- or full-time in Florida. And, the fact is, many nonresidents care about what happens in Florida. That's why they help, I believe. I don't think wind of any strength could ever remove the love so many have for the beaches of Florida.

If a hurricane strikes in September, as they historically do, tourists want to know if they will still be able to visit as planned in February or March. Typically, they can. Sometimes an alternative hotel or resort is required in the same year, but chances are that most of their favorite restaurants and other destinations will be open for business.

Florida is a place where traditions are formed and memories are made for many families over generations, and no hurricane will erase that. It's rather like sand-castles. It's the sun, sand, and sea that makes the real castle. Structures can be washed away overnight but will be rebuilt the next day with the help of those who built the previous versions. It's about family, friends, and nature—not roofs and walls.

Restoration of our home was a tremendous success. In fact, it is now being promoted as a "Mid-Century Modern Masterpiece," and that's accurate in my opinion. Hurricane Irma struck the Florida Keys on September 10, 2017. We purchased the property in November of that same year. The pool was all but destroyed, an adjacent "pool room" was ripped completely off the home, windows were shattered, air conditioners were broken beyond repair.

What was a glorious park-like setting when we first toured the property prior to the hurricane became just a snarl of fallen trees and branches.

The main areas of the house provided something of a concrete bunker with a fabulous original design and location, so we could see our way past the work ahead. It was a dreamlike place to live once restored. We both worked so hard that we didn't have a great deal of spare time, but when we did, we could walk and enjoy ourselves enough on the property itself.

It's fair to say respite was just beyond the back-door. Palms and paths were lit to create a resort-like atmosphere, and the calming sound of gently moving water came from either the pool or waterfront. We had a campfire near the beach and a private, protected boat slip to use so we could get on the water without delay.

It was a quiet community, far removed from what became country and world-wide chaos during ridiculous Covid lockdowns and mandates. Florida remained, to some degree, one of the few sane pockets of existence in the world, but it was and still is under attack from those who would like to frighten citizens into forfeiting their own God-given freedoms. Big Pine Key, with a total area of just 10 square miles and a population in 2020 of 4,521, seemed to provide another layer of protection.

As the workforce changed drastically throughout America, our business took off and wasn't showing any signs of slow down unless we couldn't staff Fleet Clean outlets and jobs fast enough. "Non-Essentials" were being sent home and handed "free" money in the name of health and safety, and just what exactly was considered a non-essential worker was not well defined to any extent.

To us, all of our clients and employees were essen-tial. We kept hiring, training, and begging people to show up at work and on time. But our government did a good job of frightening everyone into staying home to "prevent the spread," so, it was no easy trick.

While trying to build additional locations, we faced many obstacles from those who seemed, and still do seem, hellbent to stifle the very things that make Western Civilization hum—ingenuity, freedom, entrepreneurship, energy, and the hard-driving work ethic that made America both possible and great.

Particularly sad was seeing the number of small businesses that were forced to limit the number of customers they could serve, or close altogether. Our continued efforts were absolutely essential to the number of families we supported through employment. Those of us who continued to keep up with travel and physical meetings could see Main Streets throughout America bleeding lost revenue.

There was another obstacle, and that was the distance between Big Pine Key and what became our natural headquarters, Melbourne. Melbourne is also beautiful and was the home of a key employee who became only more and more valuable with increased expansion of the business. Even with an airplane and my own pilot's license, getting around Florida isn't always easy. Tropical conditions are notoriously unpredictable, particularly on a thin line of islands, or "keys."

We kept the plane at a small airstrip on Marathon Key in Marathon, Florida. That sounds like it must be a very significant place for all the repetition of "Marathon," but it's just another key, about 30 miles away from Big Pine Key by car. Like many areas throughout the keys, there's only one way to get to most places by car and everyone is subject to the speed of the cars ahead of them over long bridges. While crossing several bridges is necessary to get to Marathon Key, most notable is "Seven Mile Bridge," which really is just short of seven miles long at 6.79 miles in length. It feels like at least 21 miles long—or half a day—when driving from one end to the other.

To complicate things a bit further, most people driving through the keys are tourists. They're not driving to get somewhere quickly—they're driving to see things and read restaurant signs to help them determine their next stop. If some dolphins start dancing within view of a bridge, be prepared to stop!

So, we'd fly or drive to commute, depending on weather conditions. We worked remotely at times, but as owners, it's unwise to not show up on location whenever possible. The difference in travel time was 30 minutes to the airfield followed by an hour and twenty minutes in the air; or a complete car commute of well over five hours. Not quick enough, either way.

We were a bit melancholy about abandoning our piece of art in paradise on Big Pine Key, but moving to Melbourne was most certainly the right thing to do. Our truck washing business took off like lightning, and two additional franchises were being put together in its wake.

12

MEET THE MARSUPIALS

WE WERE STILL BUILDING Fleet Clean as fast as we could, and not as fast as companies with large fleets of trucks would have liked. After franchising the business model, we quickly became the second largest provider of truck washing services in the country. That activity attracted the private equity firm that already owned the largest provider, Fleet Wash. After negotiations, we sold the company for a life changing sum in 2018.

Instead of being caught wondering what to do next, our next business was already well-established on paper. Koala Insulation, also an eventual franchise, was first launched in two pilot locations, Panama City, Florida, and Atlanta, Georgia. While the business was very different from washing trucks, the practices that brought success were not. We had no special technology or new type of insulation, but we had a winning model that focused on reliability and customer service.

Both pilot markets showed tremendous success and we were able to pack the results into a franchise offering. When something works, people are confident about how successful they could be grabbing a set of reigns on their own. Most people love the greatest amount of freedom they can squeeze out of life, and a franchise offers an opportunity to drive your own train using something that has already been proven to have both sufficient demand, and reliable performance, that can be sold at a meaningful profit. Franchising is a way to be in business for yourself, but not by yourself. You still have the safety net of the Franchisor to help when you hit an unexpected problem.

Consumers are bombarded with ads for products. Most consumers conduct a considerable amount of research before contracting or buying anything today. Tools are at their fingertips, and they don't trust or want anyone banging on their door in an attempt to sell them anything. It's truly easy for today's consumers to compare product ratings online and determine what is the best for them within their budget.

In construction or insulation, the problem comes when trying to find the most reliable contractor to do the work. Few find the best insulation online, buy it, and install it themselves. So, it's all about the people. As Ronald Reagan famously said, "People are policy." He was absolutely correct. Without the right people, a product used in construction is just a mass of material. So much can go wrong without proper installation, and honest mistakes are sometimes made in the process of installation or ordering.

To find success, we focused almost exclusively on what could go wrong and how our company would fix anything that did. That's another thing our government never seems to care about—concentrating on the unintended consequences of everything they do. Worse, they try to do everything, including things we don't want them to do, such as choose a school for our children or mandate that we wear masks for no proven scientific or health reason.

When a company or politician fails to ask the most important questions before moving forward, you know they are not truly interested in serving you. They are not prepared for the unintended consequences, rarely admit them, and do little or nothing to fix them. Instead, they blame other factors or people for any shortcomings.

It's all about people and customer service. If not enough or too much insulation arrived at a job site, or something wasn't properly sealed, we didn't waste one second trying to avoid taking responsibility. Our job was to fix the problem as quickly as possible. There was no huffing about how the truck driver, stocker, or installer was to blame—our company was to blame, and we would be sure to resolve the problem. That's all. It's common sense.

But again, common sense is uncommon today, and it seems nearly non-existent in the halls of Congress. If a problem is discovered there, you can bet your bottom dollar only one "solution" will be proposed—a request for more appropriations from tax dollars to address the problem. And you can expect whatever problem is addressed with that additional money to grow worse.

Because our focus was customer service, most of what we did was train people. Training was required for anyone who wanted to operate their own franchise. It wasn't just a few hours either; it was a commitment of time, energy, and mental exercise. We didn't allow people to simply write a check in order to receive a tool kit or guidelines. We required franchise owners to know and understand every aspect of our product and methods. We didn't want to just take their money; we wanted them to succeed. Success is a magnet. It makes new sales for smart companies.

Americans are hardworking people, historically, and don't want to see their hard-earned money wasted. Talk to any home or business owner about what they hate the most about managing their home or business, and they'll likely list "throwing money out the window" in the top three. Government corruption will likely be in the top three also, perhaps as number one. But it's hard for individuals to fight government corruption. What they can do is try to reduce the amount of money they pay to utilities for much needed heat or air conditioning by making facilities more efficient.

It wasn't long before Koala Insulation took off and was available in several states. Our system was in place and operating smoothly. That's when it made sense to also offer more efficient windows with the same focus on customer experience. Wallaby Windows was born in 2022, and the same business model was applied. Marsupials make for good mascots!

Wallaby pilot locations also proved successful, and we had just begun offering franchises to eventual business owners in 2023 when another private equity firm that had been studying the potential of Koala Insulation came along and bought both companies at once. Koala was already a national success and one of the fastest growing franchise brands in the world. While we had really only just gotten off the blocks with Wallaby, the business model and training programs adopted from Koala Insulation were already proven and highly sought after.

During a spell of that same period, beginning in October of 2022 and lasting until February of 2023, I had also accepted an appointment to serve as an prosecutor for the State of Florida. There was a vacancy and temporary need, so when asked, I accepted the position to serve as an Assistant State Attorney. My responsibilities to our companies were becoming easier so I had the time, and I wanted to again serve in a public capacity. I truly wasn't expecting such financial success relatively early in my life, but now that I'd found it and was relieved of childhood fears of perhaps not being able to achieve financial security, I was in a position to split my time and concentration between business and public service.

Things happened quickly. Suddenly I was prosecuting criminals, something I've always deemed important. My intelligence and analytical skills were being put back to use and I was using another section of my legal training. As much as I enjoyed serving as a prosecutor for the state, ultimately I came to believe there was much more that I could do as a public servant. It seemed to me that there were many others well equipped to carry out the work needed in the offices of the State Attorney.

The satisfaction that I felt from once again serving in a public capacity changed to a feeling of obligation and conviction that I was in a position to do more. While Scott agreed to stay with the buyers of our companies on a contractual basis for the sake of business continuity, I did not. That's the very reason I never took a very visible role in the first place—so that I wouldn't become part of some future acquisition deal. Scott wanted to keep doing what he'd been doing, he loves solving business problems. I was free as a bird to move onto another chapter in my life, and find new problems to solve.

13

TURNING POINT

AS I EXPLAINED EARLIER, I've always thought that once you find success, it's important to turn around and do something for the benefit of others—to give back, as so many describe it. People give back in a variety of ways. Some make contributions to charitable causes, some volunteer time or donate items to help those in need. Often times, giving back is done informally and not connected to any organization. Sometimes it's merely people helping other people, and the only people who know about it are those involved in the transaction. Every contribution is important and helps to strengthen communities and individuals in America.

Decisions about how anyone chooses to give back to society are personal. After much thought, my decision is to now return to public service. Many people don't think of public service as a contribution. Most think of it as reaching a position of privilege, high pay, and guaranteed benefits, because that's what citizens see in the behaviors of so many holding public office. What's worse, they know their tax dollars are footing the bill. Citizens also see many public servants become wealthy while in office, and we've all been witness to what today is widespread corruption among government officials. Aside from the corruption, some elected officials are absolutely ineffective and unproductive. It's not supposed to be that way.

Not all politicians and civil servants are corrupt or unproductive, but good representatives are certainly in the minority. If that were not the case, we wouldn't see so much senseless legislation and spending by our government. It's also true that we don't have enough statesmen who truly understand what is required to be a public servant. Otherwise, we wouldn't see the lack of performance along with a regular smattering of ethics violations and unprofessional behavior. Certainly, corruption is worse than nonperformance. It's fair to say we have too many laws to begin with, so who wants mediocre minds writing more of them? It is also apparent that some of the most important laws escape enforcement.

Every public position is a privilege because it is an honor, a pledge, and a promise to serve the people, and to do it with honesty and integrity in every capacity. Few elected officials today exhibit such traits. These are not supposed to be positions for those who expect to be treated like royalty because they think they're special. Service is supposed to be a sacrifice and commitment, a duty to citizens and to our country. That's how I view the responsibility of every elected, appointed, and hired government employee—they are to be public servants, not personalities pining for positive news coverage and elite party invitations.

Like many Americans, I am frustrated, appalled, and even angered by the lack of accountability in government, while waste and corruption constantly increase at the expense of America. Because there are many in Congress who don't make sound decisions, we get stuck with policies that don't resemble the will of the people and often don't make sense. They are concocted, self-serving, money dumping attempts at social engineering falsely guised today under the names of "science," "health," or "climate change," all of which are used to push fear upon people, and none of which hold any real truth or accuracy. They're power and money grabs.

With our country currently over $33 trillion in debt, every initiative involves more spending for things that have nothing to do with the best interest of America or the will of the people. We're handing out billions to foreign countries each year while our infrastructure crumbles, our culture erodes, and our future generations are increasingly burdened with compounding consequences. No other countries are taxing their citizens to send us money.

You don't even have to be *smarter than a fifth grader,* to quote the once popular show, in order to know there is something foolish and dangerous about spending well beyond your means. It's actually the fifth graders of today and their children who will have to live with the future pain caused by the reckless spending habits of Congress. Most of the current

Senators will not live long enough to face the consequences of the policies they enact.

Few officials and representatives seem to care. In fact, they seem empowered by this fact. It's even difficult to distinguish many Republicans from Democrats today. What happened? Is a consistent majority of our Congressional representatives truly that terrible with money, or is there something more? Are more of them taking bribes than has already come to light? Are they being threatened?

Just what level of force, coercion, or ignorance causes such foolish, complicit behavior by those who claimed to be for personal responsibility, freedom, and smaller government?

At this writing, we can't even be sure that our elections are fair or accurate. Citizens who question results are ostracized, even when a significant amount of evidence is presented. Those expressing concern are even punished, cancelled, or worse. So why would anyone run for office?

Because we have to have good, honest people run. If we don't fight then we've already lost. We have to fight for freedom at every turn, and on every front. That's why I decided a run for U.S. Senate. I believe that is the office in which I can be most effective. It's not the easiest path, but it's something I can do, something I'm qualified to do, and something to which I can apply my energy, business acumen, and patriotic duty for the benefit of America and freedom the world over. I'm not running for election to use it as a steppingstone for some higher office. Instead, I wish to serve where I can in order to solve existing problems, or at least provide a voice toward them for the citizens who are tired of being ignored.

Problems can sometimes seem overwhelming, but that can't stop us from working to secure the future of our republic. As just one man in Congress, I know I can't turn the ship around myself. But I can be a force, form a caucus of like-minded statesmen, actually read any bills presented, and not be shy about pointing out the flaws and fat inserted to anything that some wish to stuff down the throats of taxpayers. While I've been a very private person, I'm fully capable of speaking up and speaking loudly when needed.

I am hard-working, smart, a speed reader, a lawyer, a businessman, and I've enjoyed an amount of success that ensures I cannot be bought, bribed, or intimidated. I won't ignore truth, and I don't like wasting anyone's time or money. That's the kind of representative people deserve, and that's what I'm willing to do for the American people.

My commitment isn't temporary. Should this race be unsuccessful, you'll not have heard the end of me. I will continue to fight for freedom and America. I don't know what lies ahead. The sea is forever changing. But I can tell you what snares and snakes I will look out for moving forward and describe the things I hold most dear—the reasons I feel compelled to enter politics and the immediate dangers I believe we face as a country and civilization—in the next few chapters.

14

FIRST THINGS

HOLDING A PRIOR ELECTED position is not really necessary in order to successfully be elected and lead. What is necessary is a solid understanding of our country's founding and the principals of that all-important, unique founding. It also seems important for lawmakers to understand law. Many of our elected officials have made it repeatedly clear that they have no understanding of either. That's unfortunate, and one wonders then why they'd want to compete for a position for which they're obviously unqualified.

Every piece of legislation should be weighed against the Constitution and the first principles of governing. They're not. I'm just one person, and if elected will be just one of 100 in the U.S. Senate, but every member gets numerous opportunities to speak, write, and vote. More members need to use those opportunities to reflect upon truth and remind the larger body, along with many citizens, of the soundness and wisdom our founders worked painstakingly to include in what is the backbone of our country.

Honesty and integrity are required to be humbled by the founding documents which guide us, and the sacrifices made by many to secure them. A statesman was never intended to be a celebrity, to grandstand, or to advance their own agenda. Instead, they are stewards and representatives chosen to advance the will of the people within the confines of our Constitution.

Human nature has not changed since the wisdom and writings of Aquinas, Aristotle, or Plato. Truth doesn't change, nor does logic or how to derive reason from logic and rationalization. The only thing that has changed is that fewer and fewer individuals are aware of or have read some of the greatest thinkers who ever lived or applied logic. Happily, it's clear that our founders read them and incorporated such truths into the charter document that governs our country. How else would the words and ideas of some of the world's greatest philosophers become mirrored in our Declaration of Independence, Constitution, and Bill of Rights?

What went into the development of these documents is even more astounding. The Federalist Papers, a series of 85 essays to promote the ratification of the Constitution, is a work of thought and art. It is a debate in print conducted by some of the finest young minds our country has ever known—Alexander Hamilton, James Madison, and John Jay—which can be found today published in its entirety as a book. The authors used the collective pseudonym of "Publius," (presumably to protect themselves from a version of what we still experience today—less-than-free speech and forms of "cancel culture"). They were brilliant, and sadly, operating high above the reading and comprehension ability of today's average readers.

Back then, the words were studied with great comprehension by nearly everyone who could read. The debates were lively, thoughtful, and important. They were honest and conducted out of a passion for what they hoped would emerge as a country that was structured to foster freedom and create the greatest country on earth. They were successful. Now it's our job to keep the Republic.

Indeed, the founders were philosophers themselves. They were also statemen. So many safeguards were deliberated and adopted by Washington, Hamilton, Franklin, John and Sam Adams, Jefferson, Madison, Jay, and others who played important roles. They didn't come to agreement easily or take matters lightly, for they all held the same concerns of factions forming among parties, power grabs, corruption, and all those things which are inescapable given the nature of man. They were fully cognizant of the fact that guarding against abuse of power, which truly does corrupt, was essential.

For our experiment in liberty to survive the test of time, layers of checks and balances along with other prescribed remedies were in order. Although they're in place, few people know it. Sometimes the checks and balances that are to be applied are swept under the rug as another means of manipulation and maladministration by less than admirable elected officials and agency appointees. The American people are not stupid, but some who have become intoxicated by power believe they are, and treat them as such by intentionally working to game the system rather than taking their direction from "we the people" and our Constitution.

Formal training isn't really required for most people to understand the principals of our founding. They learn it from their parents, their pastors, their neighbors, and others who eventually provide young minds with common sense. The teachings of our parents and grandparents allow most people to develop their own moral compass—and no, that doesn't mean they can have their own "truths." The truths remain the same, within a moral fabric.

Many people believe our Constitution is a pamphlet that can readily fit in a shirt pocket. That's because some elected officials brag about carrying a copy around and flash it in front of cameras when opportunities arise. That little pocket version is really just an outline of what exists today, and understanding what it means is published in a five volume, annotated set. The principles and Articles or clauses are in the pocket version, but the writing, references, amendments, and laws that support it cannot be understood from the souvenir version. Understanding what it means takes considerable scholarly effort, and as Justice Clarence Thomas so aptly explained, "It says what it says and it doesn't say what it doesn't say."

Many things about the U.S. Constitution and how our government was designed to function are extremely special. Of all written charters throughout the world, ours has survived the longest. Yet, our country is still relatively young, and so this experiment in liberty is still underway. We should all strive to make it survive in perpetuity. I'm not alone in believing the reason it has withstood the test of time, as compared to those of other countries, is the very things that make it unique: that our government derives its power from "*we the people*;" that all citizens have certain inalienable rights; and that our Founding Fathers saw fit to provide for the separation of powers within the legislative, executive, and judicial branches.

Consider just the Preamble to our Constitution. From that alone, the purpose of our government is abundantly clear:

"We the People of the United States, in Order to form a more perfect Union, establish Justice, insure domestic Tranquility, provide for the common defence, promote the general Welfare, and secure the Blessings of Liberty to ourselves and our Posterity, do ordain and establish this Constitution for the United States of America."

While language changes to some degree over time, the words used in our founding documents are not ambiguous. Some reprints of the original preamble above use "defense" instead of the British spelling "defence," and use "ensure" instead of the original "insure." But the meaning hasn't changed and is clear. Further in this chapter, you will see excerpts of the Declaration reprinted and may wonder about misspellings. I'm working from the original text as on file in the Library of Congress. What looks like typos are merely obsolete spellings of the same words we use today.

We are a nation under God. All of our laws rest below a higher authority. Those who may not believe in God, can take comfort in this structure also because it is what ensures our human rights and freedoms. Put another way, human rights are the rights we were born with that should never be taken away by governments. Our rights to *life, liberty, and the pursuit of happiness,* for example. The founders were all believers in God and most people in the country are, too. These are rights we possess because we are human. Religious people believe they are made in the image and likeness of God. Non-religious people may not be inclined to recognize a higher being, but they can't deny they are human. They are human and should not be subjected to any violations of human rights.

Unfortunately, our Constitution is under constant attack. That's because we are subject to the nature of man, as positions within government are filled by people, and people are not as reliable as the words of any charter. Many people around the globe and some right here in America do suffer violations of human rights. Our Constitution forbids such, but it's our job to defend and uphold the Constitution. Good character, wisdom, and good will are required to govern anything. Some see America as a prize they covet for their own aspirations. Attacks upon our Constitution come in every form imaginable, including bills written by lawmakers who try to steer our country in another direction, judges legislating from the bench, and executives engaging in pay-to-play schemes.

This is exactly what our Founders imagined and warned of, and why they so painstakingly developed and ratified the Constitution. Even after it was ratified, their concerns added the first ten amendments—the "Bill of Rights."

Aside from those documents, I must say that, in my opinion, some of the most beautiful prose ever written became part of our Declaration of Independence. Imagine the beauty and power of these poetic and true words:

> *"When in the Course of human events, it becomes necessary for one people to dissolve the political bands which have connected them with another, and to assume among the powers of the earth, the separate and equal station to which the Laws of Nature and of Nature's God entitle them, a decent respect to the opinions of mankind requires that they should declare the causes which impel them to the separation.*

There's more beauty to be read here:

> *'We hold these truths to be self-evident, that all men are created equal, that they are endowed by their Creator with certain unalienable Rights, that among these are Life, Liberty and the pursuit of Happiness.--That to secure these rights,*

Governments are instituted among Men, deriving their just powers from the consent of the governed, --That whenever any Form of Government becomes destructive of these ends, it is the Right of the People to alter or to abolish it, and to institute new Government, laying its foundation on such principles and organizing its powers in such form, as to them shall seem most likely to effect their Safety and Happiness.'

And in this document, the *rubber truly hits the road* and truth and courage don't hide, as the conditions that warrant a revolution are outlined in the Declaration of Independence. While many people have read the document and some have well-known portions of it committed to memory, consider how relevant the following statement is today:

"But when a long train of abuses and usurpations, pursuing invariably the same Object evinces a design to reduce them under absolute Despotism, it is their right, it is their duty, to throw off such Government, and to provide new Guards for their future security..."

It is evident how deeply our forefathers loved our country. How thoughtful and thorough they were during their deliberations was a such a valuable gift to each of us, and it is our duty to make sure our Constitution withstands the test of time.

The Declaration lists the numerous grievances which were the cause of the Revolutionary war, costing the lives of over 7000 Patriots between 1775 and 1783. That may not seem like a high number compared to later wars, but there weren't that many people populating the newly formed colonies, and some were still loyal to the British Crown. The population of all 13 colonies in 1775 was about 2.5 million, and roughly half a million of them were slaves. Patriots were greatly outnumbered by the well-organized soldiers of Great Britain who were loyal to a country with a population of about 8 million.

What's striking about the list of grievances contained in the Declaration is just how many similarities there are to what we've witnessed in American politics and governance today, especially regarding a government that does not truly work for the people.

Although the Patriots faced a tremendous challenge, they were highly motivated. Their sentiment can be summarized in the words famously delivered to the Second Virginia Convention by Patrick Henry in 1775 during his successful efforts to persuade colonists to fight for their freedom: "Give me liberty, or give me death." As reflected in his remarks, colonists believed in divine intervention, providence, and that God and his angels were on their side.

It seems that their beliefs were well-founded, as against all odds, a free country was born. It's not difficult to imagine how strong was their faith, for the pursuit and protection of religious and other freedoms were largely the reasons they fled Britain in the first place.

It's for many of these same reasons that we must continue to be willing to fight to protect and defend freedom. While Civil War is a subject often revisited in some circles today, it should be our last course of action. Another way to fight corruption and tyranny is to continue to encourage honest people to run for office, and for others to support them. "We the people" certainly have the power to govern this land and to govern our elected officials, but we must do it with our voices and our actions. If that fails, we certainly need to take other measures. But currently, the corrupt establishment is doing a very good job of destroying their own credibility, and we must continue to expose their hypocrisy.

It's also critical that we secure our elections. I know there are many vulnerabilities and that many people are diligently working on fixing them. That, too, is an uphill battle when obvious anomalies and statistical impossibilities are ignored, but we must continue the work and each must do their part. What I can do is throw myself into the ring to add a voice of reason and integrity along with my support for the many unsung heroes among the American citizenry.

While we outnumber those who don't respect our culture, laws, or founding, we need to work to outnumber those who hold office and other positions of power and influence, yet who continually work to undermine our beautiful country as an all-out attack upon Western civilization and civil society.

There is a wealth of talent and wisdom in America today. One needs to only read and follow some of our greatest thinkers, writers, and researchers. But given today's political climate, many of the best have been censored. Yet, it doesn't take much for us to find them. Some—both living and posthumously—have armies of followers, including Thomas Sowell, Milton Freedman, Margaret Thatcher, Ronald Reagan, and many others.

We need to shine a light on the teachings of those who have been proven right over time, and wrongfully shunned by popular culture and media for ill-conceived political agendas. We need to restore optimism, rule of law, and freedom for all Americans. This is necessary for the well-being of not only Americans, but for all people around the globe.

15

CONSTITUTIONALISM AND STATESMANSHIP

IN 1828, AMERICA'S EDUCATOR, Noah Webster, published the American Dictionary of the English Language. In that same year, Webster wrote a concise and frequently reprinted one paragraph "Biography" of George Washington:

> Literary power and statesmanship were combined in George Washington, the greatest political leader of his time and also the greatest intellectual and moral force of the Revolutionary period. Everybody knows Washington as a quiet member of the Virginia Assembly, of the two Continental Congresses, and of the Constitutional Convention. Few people realize that he was also the most voluminous American writer of his period, and that his principles of government have had more influence on the development of the American commonwealth than those of any other man.

For those unfamiliar with the writings of Washington, let me highly recommend a reading of his Farewell Address of 1796. As he delivered it upon his decision to not run for a third term as President at the age of 64 and prior to his death at 67, it's a bit like starting at the end. But there are many reasons it's an important place to start. While he was an extremely active contributor to what eventually was ratified as our constitution and all of the debates and correspondence leading to the final document as then ratified, his farewell address is a roadmap to sound statesmanship and policy that is filled with warnings of the ongoing diligence that would be required from each of us in order to keep the republic.

In it, he addresses and cautions citizens regarding many of the problems we see today which were anticipated by nearly all of our founding fathers. While I understand that not every citizen is inclined to read detailed histories of our founding that include speeches and correspondence, much of it should be required reading for anyone who aspires to serve as a public servant. To do otherwise is similar to tinkering with a fine engine without bothering to understand how it was designed to work in the first place.

Washington warns us regarding tendencies that should be kept in check on both domestic and foreign policy fronts, of the importance of fiscal responsibility, and of the delicate balance required to define the union as separate from the autonomy of individual states. He defines the importance of the separation of powers and why each level and branch of government ought to refrain from the usurpation of rights and responsibilities that lay outside of their chartered roles.

He even warns of political parties growing too big and too powerful to keep an ear toward the voice of the people and an eye on protecting our constitution and individual rights. Washington and the other founders of this nation were clearly concerned about the reality of the old adage, "power corrupts, and absolute power corrupts absolutely." Foreign policy is also mentioned in the Farewell Address with words of caution toward alliances that form groups of friends and foes:

> The nation which indulges towards another a habitual hatred, or a habitual fondness is in some degree a slave. It is a slave to its animosity or to its affection, either of which is sufficient to lead it astray from its duty and its interest. Antipathy in one nation against another disposes each more readily to offer insult and injury, to lay hold of slight causes of umbrage, and to be haughty and intractable, when accidental or trifling occasions of dispute occur.

One of my favorite passages in the speech discusses fiscal responsibility and is rather something of a pre-curser to a phrase later coined and made popular by Ronald Reagan: "Peace through strength." It really addresses another aspect of foreign policy while also reminding everyone how the use of tax dollars should be conducted with utmost respect and prudence:

> As a very important source of strength and security, cherish public credit. One method of preserving it is to use it as sparingly as possible, avoiding occasions of expense by cultivating peace, but remembering also that timely disbursements to prepare for danger frequently prevent much greater disbursements to repel it, avoiding likewise the accumulation of debt, not only by shunning occasions of expense, but by vigorous exertion in time of peace to discharge the debts which unavoidable wars may have occasioned, not ungenerously throwing upon posterity the burden which we ourselves ought to bear.

While acknowledging that future tensions will arise and are unavoidable given the nature of man, Washington urges strict adherence to the Constitution and explains that if any changes are deemed necessary in the future, only the proper course for making those changes, as also outlined in the document, should be taken. Put another way, laws create order out of chaos only if they are respected and followed by everyone. To do otherwise is to covet power only to have more of it, which is obviously not in the best interest of the people or the republic and leads to the eventual destruction of free governments.

This is also a way to begin to define statesmanship as something of a code of ethics and mutual respect that is required to conduct oneself as a public servant. To serve honorably, good character and sound judgment are required. Washington describes religion and morality as indispensable supports to prosperity and human happiness. Morality is what directs your ability to make distinctions between right and wrong. We don't see enough of that being exercised among our current leadership. Rather, just as Washington warned, we see power grabs and a lack of respect for rule of law and justice.

To turn the tide in Washington D.C., we need more people who understand and lead according to the carefully crafted document that first formed this union of states. Former Speaker of the House, Newt Gingrich, brought this need to center stage with his "Contract with America" in 1994. Just how far we waivered from the basic tenants of our Constitution was mirrored in the succinct ten summaries of proposed legislation that would be put forth by Republicans. The proposals were clear, concise, and on point. At the time it was proposed by Gingrich during a press conference on the steps of the Capital, Republicans held a minority position in the House, as they had for all of 40 years prior. Soon, all but four Republican representatives signed the Contract to which they pledged their support. Six weeks later, Republicans captured a sweeping victory, gaining a majority in the House of Representatives. Gingrich was then elected Speaker.

Statesmanship requires wisdom and intuition. Gingrich then had his finger on the pulse of the American people and knew without question that it was important to restore bonds of trust between citizens and their elected officials. It was important to spell out exactly what you planned to attempt to achieve without fine print or in-speak. The objective was to say what you're going to do, then do it. This approach not only wowed voters who flipped the power in Congress, but it also carried 20 new Republican governors to victory. Newt got to the "why" of the problem and outlined methods to fix the problems.

Of course, the proposals were met with all kinds of opposition and accusations, but they were largely successful. Things got better in America. Budgets were balanced. Crime was addressed, and welfare was reformed to promote and strengthen families. Social Security recipients were set up to keep more of their earnings and earn more in any year if they chose to continue working. These improvements in quality of life for citizens became reality because every proposal was held up to the Constitution and the goals set within it. Usurpation of power was stomped upon by representatives who listened to their constituents and exercised statesmanship.

As Reagan famously said, it was once again "morning in America." Citizens had hope that government would be held accountable, real problems were being addressed, and Washington, DC. was again a beacon of hope and a "shining city on a hill." We'd seen a great victory under Reagan with the crumbling of the Berlin Wall in 1989, which set millions of people free of from the chains of slavery under communism. And we finally had leaders who were going to concentrate on the restoration of freedoms for the American citizens who had borne the brunt of the long cold war, crippling domestic policies, and liberal agendas that had creeped up through cracks to form chains around their own necks during that same period.

16

LANE CHANGE—MOVING FROM LEFT TO RIGHT

MANY CHILDREN EMBRACE THE Democrat party prior to full maturity. That's because the democrats pretend to be caring, altruistic, and inclusive. They pretend to want to make the world a perfect place, a fair place, a utopia filled with warmth, love, generosity, peace. World peace. A place where peace and love are made available to every person and every homeless puppy. Their mantra suggests that someday, everyone will earn enough money to buy whatever they want, eat well, enjoy advancements in technology, and be part of a world where nobody has anything to worry or complain about anymore.

What part of that would not be attractive to a young person who has witnessed inequity, poverty, sorrow, crime, and conflict? It all sounds so beautiful and ideal. Besides, so many prominent Democrats are people we admire and emulate. They're rock stars, movie stars, fashion models, and fiction writers. The concept of equity being confused with the fact that "all men are created equal with certain unalienable rights" also became twisted and advanced in churches and synagogues that increasingly got caught in the fast lane to confuse congregations.

It all sounded good and true, but it wasn't. Before figuring all of this out, I even ran for a political office as a Democrat, at the level of statehouse in Georgia. I'm so glad I lost that one, as I wouldn't want to be associated with the Democrat party today. I'm not stupid, not by any stretch. But most young people are idealistic and think that if we just go along, everyone will get along, and the world will be a better place. It's also unfortunate that Democrats use that title, as it is readily confused with the term "democratic" (small "d"), and they use this to be the condescending creatures they've become.

When I was in my twenties, the Democrats strongly supported southern farmers and were focused on funding quality public education. I shared that vision. But in the years that followed, Obama was elected. Our nation became more divided and despite promising to repeal the unconstitutional, warrantless mass surveillance of US citizens, he expanded spying programs further, eroding the protections we should have under the fourth amendment.

It became clear that despite the marketing efforts to portray the democrat party as idealists who love everyone, they were actually focused on undermining individual liberties and creating a society dependent on government. If fact, nearly every government program today is designed to create dependency and compliance through an unbelievable amount of spending and wealth redistribution which is recycled as a reward for good behavior with many strings attached. This wrong-headed style of governance is actually an assortment of controls, not freedom. It makes everyone poorer, then dangles treats before the needy in exchange for compliance to behavioral goals set by power hungry, manipulative elites.

And it's true they've "become" condescending. I'd be all for bringing back the "Blue Dogs" from a time when the Democrat party was earnestly seeking improvement to governance and the quality of life for all citizens. But they're largely extinct. The Democrat party I knew as a child was hijacked. It's unrecogniz-able. I haven't changed so much, but the party of "D" certainly has over the past few decades.

That truth again hit home in spades when I saw Hillary Clinton joining other Democrats in efforts to change the meaning of the Second Amendment of our country's Constitution. Hillary declared that she believed the decision of the Supreme Court in District of Columbia v. Heller was incorrect and the Democrat party became a divisive and Marxist enterprise that seems bent on undermining the very values our nation was founded upon.

Heller is the case which clarified that the Second Amendment applied to individual possession of fire-arms, not possession only by state militias, as some anti-gun liberals had argued. They tried to assert that "the right to bear arms" only applied to militias. In other words, individuals did not have such a right to defend themselves or their property. The wicked witch, formerly of the West Wing as First Lady, was running on her husband's coattails against Donald Trump. I jumped ship and voted for Trump in 2016 and 2020, and I endorse his candidacy today.

Just think of what Hillary Clinton was trying to assert regarding the *Heller* decision in 2008: individuals were not meant to be included in our Second Amendment and right to bear arms. Really? So, only militias could keep weapons in the event our government became tyrannical and needed to be put in check? We'd only have arms available in locked cases within locked buildings of Moose and Elk halls or similar fraternities? Did she not understand that individuals make up those fraternities and associations, which is our right, as is our right to freedom of association? Just whom did she imagine makes up militias? Committees, sub-committees, and government agencies, perhaps?

Home defense, hunting, and farming are still necessary and integral parts of American life. Guns are required for these things and Hillary, along with anti-gun activists, are overstepping their bounds when they interfere with the rights of all citizens. This condescending, top-down approach to controlling all free people is highly distasteful and downright dangerous, in my opinion.

A combination of these sorts of straws coming from Democrats in Congress and elsewhere, broke this camel's back! Such nonsense! Like many great

Republicans before me who initially thought they were Democrats, including Ronald Reagan and Donald Trump, I, too, left the Democrat party in the dust and have since worked to support the party of Lincoln.

Many are no angels within the Republican Party structure, I get that. George Washington warned us of parties becoming too strong and too divisive. His warnings have since all been proven valid. However, the Republican Party has become the party of patriots who believe in individual liberty and upholding our Constitution, while the Democrats have shifted even further left and espouse policies which are destructive to our nation and designed to destroy Western civilization. Freedom is essential to prosperity, and if one is not on the side of freedom, one is not an authentic American.

I am very proud to be a member of the Republican party for many years now, and I am seeking the Republican nomination for US Senate in my home state of Florida because our party needs strong leaders who will do what they say they will do and defend the freedom of American citizens while guarding their sovereignty, pocketbooks, and God given rights.

We don't need to be in the fast lane of fads and fashion. We need to be in the right lane! I will choose dangerous freedom over "safe" tyranny always. As then Governor (CA) Ronald Reagan so aptly stated in his 1967 Inaugural Address:

"Freedom is a fragile thing and it's never more than one generation from extinction. It is not ours by way of inheritance; it must be fought for and defended constantly by each generation, for it comes only once to a people. And those in world history who have known freedom and then lost it have never known it again."

His famous quote was revised and reused in various addresses, only to make the statement stronger. And he was right. Defending our civil liberties is critical to all things. I hope and pray that this generation isn't the last to enjoy freedom, but more than that, I am jumping into the lion's den to fight for it on behalf of the American people. I will be one voice, but not the only voice. Put another way, I'll be another voice, another soldier, another arm, another faithful servant.

It is our duty to remove and replace any politicians who do not serve the people. I'm a worthy replacement, and humbly ask for your support.

17

RESTORING OPTIMISM (AGAIN) IN AMERICA

MANY AMERICANS ARE DISCOURAGED today. That's understandable. It seems we've now been subjected to an intentional assault upon common sense, truth, morality, justice, and freedom. We've all witnessed riots and destruction while law enforcement was frequently told to stand down. Looting continues to go unaddressed in major cities at highly visible brand name outlets, statues are toppled with no consequences, cars are overturned, property is vandalized, and intentional fires are started. Nobody ever seems to be apprehended or prosecuted, unless they are conservatives who were trying to stop the mayhem.

It's important to remember that those who hate America want you to give up. They want you to feel helpless, to comply with nonsense, and to become dependent. Instead, think of the resilience and struggle others have overcome facing tyranny in the past. We know from our ancestors that it is possible to overcome tyranny, to expose and prosecute corruption and fraud, and to re-ignite the flame of freedom.

Freedom is required in order to pursue happiness. As such, every citizen should be poised to defend it.

Nobody can take away your God given rights. Our Declaration of Independence clearly indicates an authority higher than any man-made code or treaty. Although there are no references to God in the Constitution, our founders saw fit to translate those rights into words and ratify them as the first ten amendments to our Constitution—the Bill of Rights. Every single State in the Union also references a God as a higher authority in their Constitutions.

So, the only way our freedom can be taken from us is if we yield to hostile forces, tolerate injustice, turn a blind eye toward the erosion of our culture, and stop participating in the perennial need for every American to engage in the defense and protection of our republic. Our Constitution doesn't protect itself, and neither do massive political parties. It's up to citizens to become the guardians of our freedoms and hold politicians accountable.

Washington's historic statements warning about political parties is as relevant today as it ever was. Both of the major political parties have become seeded with politicians who can't be trusted and are so self-absorbed with their ill-gotten power that they ignore the voice of the people. This has caused many to develop complete disinterest in politics—they feel hopeless. We need to restore faith in our political processes by holding all public servants accountable.

Looking back at the conservative revolution led by Newt Gingrich in 1994, it's impossible to ignore the improvements our country enjoyed for the following six years. An important question to ask is why such progress didn't continue? The answer is similar to why institutions often fail over time—they are run by humans, and humans are fallible. In the case of the Contract with America, what happened is that statesmen who previously stood with the principles of the Contract eventually fell away from their commitment to the principles within it. Instead, many began to focus on the personal character flaws of then President Clinton, who actually announced "the end of big government" during his campaign in the wake of Republican victories.

We need more politicians who will start with and stick with conservative policies instead of getting mired in missions of character assassination. Many politicians took their eyes off the ball to focus on an affair had by President Clinton and prove him a liar on the subject. They did that in an effort to win back the office of President for their party. It served no other purpose. What was lost was more progress made on behalf of the American people. Frankly, I don't care about the party affiliation of any statesman or what they do in their private lives as long as the official actions of elected politicians are in the best interest of the people, reflect the will of the people, and are not criminal.

We must restore optimism in America, as Ronald Reagan so famously did. When Jimmy Carter issued nationwide depressants with his claim of a great malaise and looming energy crisis, Reagan turned it around with positive statements and energy. Similar to Donald Trump's "Make America Great Again" campaign slogan, Reagan focused on the positive and possible, re-energizing all honest Americans. We are not victims, but rather, we are capable human beings who cherish freedom. Reagan was also boldly honest. Who can forget his "Mr. Gorbachev, tear down that wall!" speech? Freedom is important to optimism, as optimism fuels ingenuity and is key to success. Great leaders understand this. Not-so-great leaders say things like, "it's going to be a cold, dark winter."

Attitude is so important to success in so many arenas. I know this from my experience as an entrepreneur. Nobody starts a business with the notion they are going to fail. That optimism is what hoists all business leaders above any hurdles that get in their way. The same attitude is required by statesmen. Those who lack the spirit of America are the ones who believe things are so bad that we need to control the thinking and behavior of all people. They don't trust people to make decisions for themselves, or parents to make decisions for their children. This is wrong-headed and must be battled daily to maintain our freedoms and the American dream.

Like Donald Trump, Newt Gingrich had the courage to swim upstream. Gingrich laid out his policy agenda and legislative proposals well ahead of the election in 1994. That type of strategy was always frowned upon by the world of consultants because it was thought the equivalent of "showing your cards." Put another way, if you actually tell citizens what you plan to do once in office, you are handing all media a chance to directly pick apart both you as a politician and your proposals. But what would be so wrong with that? Why not be clear and direct regarding your ideas and let them get picked apart if they are not good?

The hidden reason why some don't reveal what they really think is so they can hide their true feelings and motivations, or change them according to the direction of political winds. If that's the standard, then why not just draw the names of representatives from a hat? If none of them spell out their beliefs or agendas, on what basis do we choose our leaders? Is it how they look, the sound of their voice, the clothes they wear, or some aspect of their personal life? If that's the case, it's small wonder that we can't trust our current leaders.

We can restore faith in American politics. What's required is simply that all candidates and elected officials are pressed to say what they mean and do what they say they will do; that all proposals are held up against our Constitution; and, that corruption is not tolerated at any level. Justice must be administered quickly and equally in order to maintain peace and allow citizens to pursue happiness.

A moral compass is required in order to keep the republic. Our founders understood that. But we have failed to do our part as citizens—hold feet to the fire. It's understandable that people are consumed with their own duties, and life can get in the way of many people becoming active in politics. But it is our duty to become engaged. We are top of command when it comes to preserving our freedoms and protecting our country. While my previous public service has been a relatively small portion of my adult life, I'm now sick of sitting on the sidelines and ready to engage more fully. Of course, these are not my words, but "Now is the time for all good men to come to the aid of their country!" Everyone can do something. If you've never called or written to a representative before, I urge you to do so. Do whatever you can. Bring the common sense of the silent majority back to the front of the minds of elected officials.

It's true that one cannot be weak or poor in order to run for office. I've been blessed and am neither, so I'm jumping into the lion's den.

18

UNITED WE STAND

TO VIEW THE MEDIA landscape today, you'd think we are each more distant from our fellow Americans than ever before. I believe that simply isn't so. At the heart of most of us, we all want the same things. We want to see our families prosper and grow old together, celebrating the traditions that we hold dear, whatever those may be. We want to see our children grow up in safe neighborhoods, surrounded by infinite options that are equally available to all. We want to enjoy the fruits of our own labor and share with whom we choose. We want to love who we want and enjoy the freedoms this nation was built upon. We want to retain all rights possible while enjoying a beneficial government that works to accomplish for us all what we could not accomplish individually.

We do not seek only to benefit from each other; Americans are generous and we are willing to contribute to the betterment of all. When performed on a limited and strictly necessary scale, this isn't socialism, but simply our moral reality. We're willing to pay taxes and contribute to our government those funds it genuinely needs to accomplish basic objectives like national security and many other useful causes for which our government is truly the best means.

We're willing to save for a rainy day and delay gratification for a better tomorrow. We're willing to work towards what we know is right. We know that with great power comes great responsibility, but that this responsibility is first and foremost to our own. There are countless among us who are willing to do anything, even lay down their lives, in the service of their fellow man. This level of love is special, and it is the bedrock on which our nation is built.

None of us want to see our fellow man left behind. There are many still who cannot do for themselves, and we all want to ensure they are cared for with the same compassion we show our own families. We expect those of us who can work and benefit society to care for themselves and their family members to do so rather, than rely on others. We believe that self-reliance is the root of independence and freedom. We should guard this principle carefully. Once lost, freedom is not easily regained. Freedom is never given; it is always hard won through painful fights. We have the chance to preserve our freedoms and carefully restrain the ever-growing limitations on those freedoms, and we must take this chance before it is gone.

With the loss of self-reliance comes the loss of faith in our basic societal structure. Without self-reliance and independence, freedom is not real and we can never realize the benefits of our labor. Without the ability to realize these benefits, who among us would labor for nothing?

Where has the trust for our fellow man gone? Where has the honor and integrity that is the basis for trusting our fellow citizen gone? Some would have you believe it has all but disappeared, but I see it every day in all of the people I interact with. At their core, most people are good. We should find the good in ourselves and our fellow man, and strive to build upon this good to become ever better.

Our predecessors huddled together around fires in poorly insulated structures and dreamed that we would have the best society the world has ever known. We have lost sight of this wonderous vision while it remains right in front of us. We can accomplish so much together, and creating divisions serves no one.

Our constitutional system of governance, our great American experiment, is still very young and we hold in our hands the last and brightest hope of humanity to ensure self-determination and government by and for the people. Almost universally, we still believe in the same things upon which our constitution was founded. Despite differences and the selfish interests of some, we still believe in the freedoms which were built into that document as they were written. We still want the same things our founders did, but we have gotten off track. We can get back on track, but we must make these efforts urgently or risk the permanent extinguishment of the brightest light humanity has ever known.

Offer to your fellow man the benefit of the doubt. When offered the opportunity to cast doubt, parse words, or impart unsaid meanings, open your heart and mind with love and embrace the possibility that we are all really equal and we all really do want our nation to exist as a large, diverse, very different but very happy family.

We are better than we have been. We can accomplish more than we have accomplished. We should work to constantly improve ourselves, our nation, and the world. We can work together and lead this great nation and the world to a better tomorrow.

19

ON THE TRAIL

AT LAST, I HAVE begun my favorite part of my new venture to seek elected office—touring the state and meeting the people. Florida is my home and I shall never truly leave it. I am determined to fight for the rights, freedoms, and best interest of my beloved Florida neighbors.

In this particular election, I'm running against a man who has marketed himself as a strong conservative fighter. He says he is for cutting our government spending, protecting gun rights, and protecting our seniors through programs like social security. But when you separate his record from his rhetoric and look at his actions rather than his words, the reality is very different from his scripted lines on television.

Despite saying he is fiscally conservative, he has voted to increase our national debt by trillions of dollars. As of the writing of this chapter, he voted along with all of the democrats to avoid a government shutdown by essentially giving in to what the democrats demanded. The ongoing abdication of the power of the purse is why we are so deeply in debt. Letting the executive branch lead Congress around rather than

Congress exercising its constitutional authority to set boundaries through the budget must end if we want change in this nation's trajectory and debt levels.

Despite saying he is in favor of gun rights, when he was governor of Florida, he signed unconstitutional restrictions and red flag laws. In fact, he is held up in state legislatures around the nation by democrats who point out that even Republicans are in favor of gun control. They reference the gun restrictions he implemented in Florida as a good start towards the gun control regime they hope to enact nationally.

Despite saying he wants to protect programs like Social Security, he published a plan that proposed "sunsetting" this program with the line that "if Congress thinks it is worth keeping, they can pass it again." Considering that Congress can't agree to keep the lights on each year (nearly shutting down the government has become commonplace), my opponent thought it was acceptable to put a program that millions of seniors rely on up for debate every five years. After much animosity from both sides of the aisle, he has since modified his plan to exclude Social Security. I don't buy that act, though, because when he was governor and had the power to cut the state retirement benefits program, he did so. He doesn't hesitate to take funds from the pockets of those in need and I don't trust him to ensure the government honors its promises to the seniors who worked for decades while paying into the Social Security program with the promise they would get a return on their investment.

As for civil liberties, it's not just gun rights that my opponent is willing to sell out. Its virtually all freedoms. In March of 2020, during the COVID pandemic, my opponent released a 9-Step Plan to stop the disease. Among these steps were the suggestion that all air travel should be grounded, mandatory temperature checks, and government-enforced quarantines.

Most disturbingly, he proposed that the government should establish and enforce "containment zones." This is essentially the same plan the CCP implemented in China—they fenced in neighborhoods, shut down highways, and forced people (at gun point) to remain locked in place. Any Senator who would propose we so deeply violate the individual liberties of our citizens is obviously not honoring their oath to uphold the Constitution. The role of government should not be to force people to make the "correct" decision but rather to give them the facts and let them choose for themselves. If people choose to endanger themselves, that is their right and it is the price of liberty. I will always choose dangerous freedom over safe tyranny.

While all of these particular issues will be distant memories in the coming years, it is important that citizens vote based on careful research. If all you do is watch TV to get your information, you could be fooled by a politician like the one I'm running against. Actions speak louder than words, and I urge you to look at the actions.

Freedom is never far away from being lost. The democrat party has no interest in protecting our freedoms, or the rule of law, for that matter. The Republican party is doing better, but the examples above illustrate the importance of further change and vigilance. We must remove any politician from office when it becomes clear that they do not have the best interest of our individual liberty at heart. When they act against the wishes of the people, it is our duty to replace them. That's exactly what I'm asking voters to do in this upcoming election.

Now that I'm fresh on the campaign trail, I must say that the most awkward thing I've had to face is talking about myself. This book has been difficult. In business, I never really talked about myself at all. But, in fairness, I know that at this juncture, most of you have never heard of me. I'd be fine with that if I hadn't entered politics, but now you deserve to know more about me.

Florida is a beautiful state. Because we are a tourist destination, most people only know the famous beaches. I can't blame them. After all, if you're heading to sunny Florida to escape the cold and snow of other regions, why wouldn't you want to head for a beach? The only problem there is which of the many fabulous beaches might you visit? But I urge any who can to visit the many beautiful and interesting areas within inland areas in Florida. You'll be met with an abundance of common sense, wisdom, wildlife, lakes, diversity, and darn good food!

If you see my bus (yes, I even have an official "candidate" bus), please follow it. I want to meet you!

My favorite thing on the trail is meeting people and answering their questions. While the bus was big and expensive, it makes perfect sense because many key campaign staff can travel, plan, and prepare at the same time. I'm awfully glad I am not the driver. Not that I couldn't if I had to, but I now relish the additional time I have to think and write while enroute.

Media attention is rather new to me. Nobody ever really wanted to interview the corporate counsel of a truck washing, window, or insulation company. They surely never wanted to interview the owner of a single steak house, custom chocolate company, or healthy food restaurant that served yogurt. But here I am. I'm wonderfully delighted that I seem to have natural comfort in front of cameras and microphones. I think that stems from truly enjoying meeting and talking with people. It's as if the cameras and microphones disappear. That is a truly welcome and unexpected blessing!

Over the next several months, my calendar and social media sites will be regularly updated. Please find and follow me. And, as I mentioned previously, should this effort be unsuccessful, you'll not have heard the last of me. To serve my county, whether elected or not, is my forever goal.

With love and hope, I thank you for reading.

Go to www.keithgross.com to learn more. Follow me on social media and write to me there. I love engaging directly with all of you and will continue fighting to preserve our freedoms.

ABOUT THE AUTHOR

KEITH GROSS IS MANY things: an entrepreneur, a pilot, an attorney, and a conservative activist. But there's one thing he'll never be: a career politician.

Growing up in rural Florida shaped him into a man who understands and appreciates the American Dream and the principles of equality, liberty, and opportunity that have made this nation the greatest in the world. Because he has enjoyed them, he is determined to protect those values for generations to come.

Now, Keith Gross is running for US Senate to disrupt the status quo in Washington. He's conquered the business world through his never-quit attitude, and in the Senate, he'll represent Florida with that same determination and grit. Because that's what makes America great.